the DIRTY Version

{ON STAGE, IN THE STUDIO, AND IN THE STREETS WITH OL' DIRTY BASTARD}

BUDDHA MONK and MICKEY HESS

DEY ST.
AN IMPRINT OF
WILLIAM MORROW PUBLISHERS

DEY ST.

HarperCollins books may be purchased for educational, business, or sales promotional use. For information please e-mail the Special Markets Department at SPsales@harpercollins.com.

FIRST EDITION

Designed by Paula Russell Szafranski

Library of Congress Cataloging-in-Publication Data

Monk, Buddha.

The Dirty version : on stage, in the studio, and in the streets with Ol' Dirty Bastard / by Buddha Monk and Mickey Hess.—First edition.

    pages cm

    Includes bibliographical references.
ISBN 978-0-06-223141-3 (hardcover) 1. Ol' Dirty Bastard, 1968–2004. 2. Rap musicians—United States—Biography. I. Hess, Mickey, 1975–. II. Title.
    ML420.O536M66 2014
    782.421649092—dc23

    [B]

                                          2014011086

THE DECIDEDLY ROMANTIC IDEA IS THAT
NOT BEING ABLE TO GIVE A FUCK HOLDS
INFINITELY BOLDER POTENTIAL THAN
CHOOSING TO NOT GIVE A FUCK. DESTINY
IS DEFINITELY PART OF THE EQUATION.
SOME FOLKS ARE BORN TO BE FREE IN
THIS WAY.

—DREAM HAMPTON, ON OL' DIRTY BASTARD

MOTOR MOUTH, CLOWN OF CLASS WARFARE,
WELFARE MILLIONAIRE. . . .
YOUR CARELESSNESS REMINDS US HOW
QUICK WE ARE TO JUDGE, HOW SERIOUS
THINGS DONE BECOME. DIRTY AS THE
SOUTH, SWEET AS NEON CHERRY PIE
FILLING FROM A CAN.

—KEVIN YOUNG, FROM "ODE TO OL' DIRTY BASTARD"

Contents

Introduction

NO FATHER TO HIS STYLE

Russell Tyrone Jones was best known as Ol' Dirty Bastard of the hip-hop supergroup the Wu-Tang Clan, but before that he rapped as Ason Unique—the name his cousin Islam gave him in his teens, when he became involved with the Nation of Gods and Earths (the Five Percent Nation). Just as Cassius Clay changed his name to Muhammad Ali in 1964 when he converted to the Nation of Islam and left behind his English slave name for a righteous Arabic name, the young Russell Jones followed the Five Percenter tradition to adopt a new name that would speak for himself in English, the language he spoke every day. Jones began to go by A Son Unique, or Ason Unique. It was a name and a label that he never left behind, as he sang, shouted, and spelled out his Ason Unique in songs by the Wu-Tang Clan and in his own solo releases. The name fit: it was Dirty's uniqueness that led his fellow Wu-Tang member Method Man to explain that the group called him the Ol' Dirty Bastard because "there ain't no father to his style."

Dirty's style of rap was unique. His rhyme style ranged from drunkenly slurred to growled, crooned, and warbled to shouted, grunted, and screamed—often all within the same verse. The first time I heard Ol' Dirty Bastard's "Goin' Down" I was sure I was listening to three different rappers on the song. After a nearly one-minute intro of sustained croaking that eventually builds to a wobbling high note, Dirty begins the first verse by spelling out "Unique God" (Five Percenters often refer to each other as Gods) in a low, breathy voice that almost registers as a whisper until his voice raises in pitch and volume as he draws out the last syllable: "I'm the U-N-I, the Q-U-E, the G to the O-Deeeeeeee." Then halfway through the song he's singing "Over the Rainbow" while his wife berates him for getting with groupies.

Dirty made his recorded debut in 1992, on Wu-Tang Clan's self-released single "Protect Ya Neck," which would be included on their album *Enter the Wu-Tang (36 Chambers)*. Wu-Tang Clan—one of hip-hop's most enduring groups—emerged at a moment when hip-hop's focus was shifting from the group to the solo artist. The early nineties marked a new era of rap's solo superstars, as MC Hammer and Vanilla Ice broke the sales records set before them in the eighties by groups such as Run DMC and N.W.A. While Hammer and Ice achieved pop superstardom in 1990, contract disputes held up the release of a new Run DMC album. N.W.A broke up in 1991, and by 1992 its former members Ice Cube, Dr. Dre, and Eazy-E had each released solo albums taking shots at their former partners. Having billed themselves as "the world's most dangerous group," N.W.A broke up over the kind of monetary disputes that might end any business partnership: Ice Cube—the first member to leave—claimed that Eazy-E and the group's manager Jerry Heller were keeping an inordinate amount of N.W.A's profits for themselves, and Dr. Dre soon followed Cube out the door. Dre then left Heller and Eazy's Ruthless Records to form Death Row Records with Marion "Suge" Knight amid accusations that Suge and his soldiers had threatened Eazy with violence in order to secure Dre's release from his contract. By 1992, hip-hop had become big business, and the rappers who would excel in the next decades came to develop a business acumen that rivaled their street knowledge. Jay-Z would soon claim to have parlayed the skills he learned in the drug trade into a new approach to the music industry, but before Jay released his first record he watched the ever-strategic Wu-Tang Clan—whose members shared a fascination with the game of chess—make a legendary opening move.

Wu-Tang Clan used the success of their self-released single to leverage an unprecedented recording contract that allowed each of the Clan's nine members the freedom to record as a solo artist for any label he chose. This ingenious contract condition set the stage for Wu-Tang Clan to become hip-hop's most important new group of the nineties: as its members established successful solo careers it would only strengthen the group's brand. For the plan to work, each man in the Clan had to stand out with his own style, swagger, and star quality. Each Wu-Tang member would have to bring something unique to the table. Enter the man with no father to his style, the man who called himself Unique. Enter Russell Jones, whose personality was so big that it came to overshadow his music.

Just as there was no father to Dirty's unique style, there was no precedent for a hip-hop star to lift a burning car off a four-year-old girl, or take a limousine to pick up his family's welfare check, or escape from court-mandated rehab for a sneak appearance onstage with his group on the other side of the country—and make it out of the venue without getting arrested. Dirty shoplifted sneakers with hundreds of dollars in cash in his pocket. He sunbathed nude on a hotel balcony in Berlin. He loved taking his children to Coney Island, but he faced a judge over unpaid child support. When President Bill Clinton was proposing welfare reform to "end welfare as a way of life," Dirty used his welfare card in the cover art for his album.

Dirty quickly became disillusioned with touring and began missing studio sessions and scheduled appearances with the Wu-Tang Clan. He became so infamous for missing shows that fans were surprised when he *did* show up. Dirty succumbed to the same excesses of drugs, alcohol, and sex that lure in so many popular musicians, but at the same time he suffered from his insistence on remaining a part of the Brooklyn neighborhoods that raised him. Robberies and attempts on his life left him paranoid and convinced he was the next man to die in the series of unsolved murders of rap stars that saw Tupac Shakur and the Notorious B.I.G. shot to death in 1996 and 1997, respectively. It would seem easy enough to dismiss Dirty's theories of a government conspiracy against him, but even the cops were shooting at Dirty. In February 1999—just one day before officers from the

NYPD's Street Crimes Unit shot and killed the unarmed Guinean college student Amadou Diallo—a Brooklyn grand jury ruled that Dirty should not face charges in connection with an incident in which plainclothes officers from the same unit fired on Dirty's vehicle. Two weeks later, in California, Dirty was the first person ever arrested under a new law that made it illegal for felons to wear body armor.

A rap star for just over a decade, Dirty spent most of the last five years of his life either in court-mandated rehab facilities or in prison. The attempts on his life combined with years of cocaine use produced a profound paranoia that prison exacerbated as his celebrity called attention to him—one of the worst moves for a new inmate in a maximum-security prison. He found himself the target of his fellow inmates, who threatened and attacked him. During his final two-year prison term he signed with new management and inked a deal with Roc-A-Fella Records, the label that was home to Jay-Z and Kanye West. When Dirty died just a year later, in 2004, in the Manhattan recording studio where he was working on tracks for a comeback album, he left his family, friends, and fans to wrestle with the question of whether he had succumbed to living out the kinds of experiences that kept his name in the press. Would he be remembered more for his drug arrests than for his music?

By Dirty's side throughout all of these trials and tribulations was his friend, the producer and rapper Buddha Monk. If you've seen video footage of Ol' Dirty Bastard performing, you've likely seen Buddha Monk by his side. Buddha toured the world with Ol' Dirty Bastard and the Wu-Tang Clan. He stood next to Dirty on his first appearance on *Yo! MTV Raps* in 1995, and he performed with Dirty in his final onstage appearance with Wu-Tang Clan at the Rock the Bells festival in 2004. Along the way, responsibility fell to Buddha to get Dirty to the studio, to the video shoot, and to the show. When Wu-Tang needed to know where Dirty was, they called Buddha.

Buddha knew the Dirty who'd sneak out of a hotel at 5:45 to avoid a 6 A.M. video shoot. He knew the Dirty who'd escape the pressures and responsibilities of the music industry by leaving New York to stay with friends in Willingboro, New Jersey, where he'd hang out with Buddha and the rap crew Zu Ninjaz. It was Buddha's job to make sure Dirty's fun didn't go too far and that he knew when it was time to get back to work. At times the role put a strain on their friendship, and in the worst of his drug use Dirty would ditch even Buddha.

I first met Buddha through the rapper Traum Diggs, when I invited the two of them as guest speakers for the Hip-Hop and American Culture course I teach at Rider University in New Jersey. I'd read interviews with Buddha before, and his talk with my class confirmed that the man knew how to tell a story. He was there from the beginning. He was playing shows with Ol' Dirty Bastard before Wu-Tang Clan had released an album, and he was on set for the music video shoots after they did. Buddha worked tirelessly in the recording studio on Dirty's debut album *Return to the 36 Chambers: The Dirty Version*, and was the go-to man a decade later when Roc-A-Fella needed to see Dirty return to his old stamina and charisma on tracks for his comeback record.

As for me, I dedicated my doctoral dissertation to Ol' Dirty Bastard. You can find it in the stacks in Ekstrom Library at the University of Louisville: "To Ol' Dirty Bastard: I liked your motherfuckin' style." My years of listening to and reading about Wu-Tang and Ol' Dirty Bastard culminated in years of talking and writing with Buddha Monk to bring together this book. Like many fans, I already knew the general trajectory of Dirty's life story, but I didn't know Dirty loved broccoli on his pizza. I didn't know where Dirty felt most at home or where he was hiding between his sneak appearance with Wu-Tang in New York and his arrest six days later in Philly. In the following pages, Buddha Monk tells the story of Ol' Dirty Bastard, from their first meeting as kids on Brooklyn's Putnam Avenue to Buddha's efforts over the past decade to pick up the pieces and continue making music after the death of his close friend.

This book was written primarily from my conversations with Buddha Monk in which Buddha reminisced about his friendship with Ol' Dirty Bastard. As Buddha was working from memory rather than a recording or a transcript, the dialogue in the book is written in a way that evokes the feeling and meaning of what was said, rather than the exact words people spoke. In all instances, the essence of the dialogue remains true. I found outside sources useful in depicting the events for which Buddha was not present and—in cases such as taped interviews, performances, and court transcripts—preserving the exact words spoken. William Shaw's and Sacha Jenkins's interviews of Dirty in prison, for example, proved valuable to me in getting down Dirty's description of his mind state while behind bars. I conducted interviews with Icelene Jones—Dirty's widow and the administrator of his estate—who generously gave me her descriptions of Dirty's relationship with her and their children. I interviewed Spliff Star, Prince Paul, John "Mook" Gibbons, and Lord Digga, who contributed their memories of Dirty. Chapter 14 was greatly informed by an interview Buddha and I conducted with K-Blunt of the Zu Ninjaz. My conversations with Dr. Deanna Nobleza in Jefferson University's Department of Psychiatry and Human Behavior and Dr. Jessica Kovach at Temple University School of Medicine provided valuable insight on the effects of the antipsychotic medication Haldol, which was prescribed to Dirty in prison.

— Mickey Hess

CHAPTER 1

RUSTY

His mama called him Rusty. He was known to the world by many names: Unique Ason, Osirus, Dirt McGirt, Big Baby Jesus. All the names became part of his legend—*did you hear what that crazy Ol' Dirty Bastard is calling himself now?* But when I met him we were kids and he was Russell Jones. His mama, Miss Cherry Jones, would holler, "Rusty, get in the house! Rusty, come here for a minute." And that's what she called him when she talked to me on the phone that sad night. "He's smiling, Buddha. Rusty's laying here smiling."

It was November 13, 2004. Ol' Dirty Bastard, my friend, was dead. Dirty died two days shy of his thirty-sixth birthday. He'd served a two-year sentence for drug possession and signed a new deal with Roc-A-Fella Records the day he came out of prison. Cofounders Jay-Z and Damon Dash had built Roc-A-Fella into one of the most powerful labels in hip-hop: they'd signed Beanie Sigel, they'd signed Kanye West. But people thought they were crazy for signing Dirty. Dirty was a hip-hop legend, no question, but there were doubts about his future in the music business. He was crazy, people said. Unpredictable. He was too far gone on drugs.

Dirty had spent two of the last three years of his life in prison, and before that it was a year or more in and out of rehab. At one point, in 2000, he escaped from a rehab facility in California and showed up onstage at a Wu-Tang concert in Manhattan. Dirty made a surprise appearance at the Hammerstein Ballroom. He came onstage for "Shame on a Nigga" from Wu-Tang's first album, did a couple more songs with his crew, and told the crowd, "I can't stay on the stage too long tonight. The cops is after me. The whole fuckin' world's after me." And just like that, he disappeared. Made it offstage, through the venue, past the cops out front, and he was gone. Six days later he was arrested in Philly in a McDonald's parking lot.

They sent him in for a psychiatric evaluation, then they put him on suicide watch while he awaited sentencing. Then it was Clinton Correctional Facility, two to four years for criminal possession of a controlled substance. They put him in with the general population. Every day he was in there, there were niggas threatening to kill him. They broke his leg. They said they were gonna set him on fire in his bunk. He was in there almost two years before he was granted parole, and after that he spent three months in Manhattan Psychiatric Center before they released him back into society to work on his comeback album. A little over a year later he was gone.

In the ten years since Dirty died, I've been touring the world with my own music and I still see the impact that he had around the globe. I've seen Ol' Dirty Bastard murals painted on walls in Romania, Australia, and Russia. I had a dude I met in Italy tell me, "I learned English listening to you and Dirty rap."

"Our English is broke as fuck on those records," I told him. "How the fuck you learn English from us?"

I toured the world performing onstage with Dirty. I was there for his early shows with the Wu-Tang Clan before they had a record deal, and I was onstage performing with him at the final show he ever did with Wu-Tang, a few months before his death. Search YouTube for Dirty's drunk freestyle on *Yo! MTV Raps* or his Roc-A-Fella press conference the day he came out of prison. You see the big dude standing right next to him? That's me. That's Buddha Monk.

Most of the major events in his life that people remember, I was there. You've heard the stories: Dirty once picked up his food stamps in a limousine, Dirty lifted a burning car off a four-year-old girl in Brooklyn, Dirty was kicked out of rehab for getting drunk, Dirty stole a fifty-dollar pair of sneakers while on tour—and he had five hundred dollars in his pocket. It seems like everybody's telling *a* story instead of telling the *true* story. Dirty was a loving brother, a caring friend, and a very supportive father to his kids. Even on his bad days, no matter how bad he was, tomorrow would come and it was hard to stay mad at him, because that's just who he was. It wasn't a character. It was him.

Dirty was born in Brooklyn in 1968, the year Martin Luther King Jr. was killed and Shirley Chisholm became the first black woman elected to the United States Congress. During Dirty's early years his family moved around Brooklyn from one neighborhood to another: from Fort Greene, to East New York, to the border of Bedford-Stuyvesant and Crown Heights, where I lived. When I met Dirty I was eleven and he was twelve. It was 1980, and Dirty and I were witnessing the rise of a new form of music called hip-hop. We were living at the edge of "Do or Die" Bed-Stuy, New York's largest ghetto and the setting for Spike Lee's 1989 film *Do the Right Thing,* which would soon show the world the racial tensions at play there. We cheered when Radio Raheem walked through that movie with a boom box on his shoulder playing Public Enemy's "Fight the Power," and we were heartbroken at the end when two white cops take him out. That scene really captured the fear a lot of us had because of racial profiling and excessive force on the part of the police. In the movie the crowd sees what happens to Radio Raheem and they start chanting, "Howard Beach! Howard Beach!"—which was the name of a Queens neighborhood we all recognized. In 1986, Michael Griffith—a twenty-three-year-old black dude from Bed-Stuy—was struck and killed by a car after he was chased onto the highway by a group of white thugs screaming, "Niggers, get the fuck out of our neighborhood!" Howard Beach was over 80 percent white, and Bed-Stuy was over 80 percent black.

A lot of rappers grew up in Bed-Stuy—Mos Def, Fabolous, Lil' Kim, and Jay-Z came from there. The Notorious B.I.G. came from Clinton Hill, just a few blocks away. Dirty and I both lived near the intersection of

Putnam and Franklin Avenues. On our blocks, hip-hop was the shit. Hip-hop and house music—that was what you heard in our neighborhood. The people that lived on my block loved house music, the people on Dirty's block loved hip-hop, and we all loved our parents' music: the Chi-Lites, the Temptations, the Four Tops, the O'Jays. Fridays and Saturdays on my block were like listening parties. My man Junior Austin owned a club and he would leave his doors open at night while everybody was shooting pool, so we could hear the music coming from inside. I would be upstairs in my place spinning records. My older brother was a DJ, so I learned to DJ by messing with his equipment when he wasn't home. He'd told me never to touch his records so I used to have to put everything back just like it was so he wouldn't catch me and beat my ass.

Around the corner Dirty and his family would be out on the corner and his uncles would be showing Dirty how to dance. Everybody would just be singing and having a good time, all the aunts and uncles and cousins. I could hear them out there having fun, so one night when I was thirteen I finally had to go around the corner and hang out with them. I just sat and listened. Dirty was sitting on the stoop with his mama and sisters. Dirty loved to listen to his mother sing. That night he was sitting next to her on the stoop and said, "Mama, sing for us." The whole street got quiet. I got chills. Dirty's mother, Miss Cherry, can sing like no one else in the world. She sang Gladys Knight, Patti LaBelle. Dirty wanted to hear "When Am I Gonna Find True Love?" The uncles were dancin', grilling food, drinking a few beers, laughing, and just enjoying themselves. Uncle Pete put his hand on my shoulder and said, "Look, boy, this is what real music is. This is what life is *about*." This was what family was really about.

Dirty's parents worked hard to provide for their kids. Miss Cherry was a dispatcher for the New York City Police Department. Dirty's father, William Jones, worked for the Metropolitan Transit Authority. Even though we weren't growing up in the safest part of Brooklyn, you could say Dirty had a fairly typical American childhood. When he was little he helped his older brother on his paper route. His daddy, William, used to wake up early and take Dirty fishing out in Far Rockaway, Queens. His parents were hard workers, so it surprised Miss Cherry when Dirty came home from school one day and told her he was never going to work for anybody in his life.

Dirty's parents separated in 1984, when Dirty had just turned sixteen. His father has said that Dirty never accepted their split-up. But even after the divorce, both parents had a hand in raising him. If there was a situation with the kids they were both there, no problem. But Dirty spent more time with the Cuffie side of his family—that's Cherry's side—which is the Native American part of his ancestry. Dirty's grandfather was Chief Fred Cuffie of the Shinnecock Indians, who generations ago had owned part of New York. RZA and GZA from Wu-Tang Clan are his cousins from the Cuffie side of the family.

With Dirty coming from such a musical family and me learning to DJ, it made sense that we became friends. When we were sixteen we used to hang out at a lot of schools trying to get girls when we should have been in class at our own school. From an early age that's what me and Dirty were interested in: girls and music. We loved to listen to people rapping on Brooklyn street corners, and we loved the tapes that the groups were beginning to pass around. That's how the music spread before hip-hop was played on the radio—the groups made their own cassette tapes to sell or give out at parties they played, and the people who'd attended those parties went home and dubbed copies to pass on to their friends. Those tapes were how Dirty and I heard the hip-hop being made outside of Bed-Stuy and Crown Heights—by groups like the Cold Crush Brothers and the Fearless Four up in the Bronx and the Treacherous Three up in Harlem. We also loved the first rap records that the labels released: the Sugarhill Gang, the Funky Four Plus One, and Kurtis Blow. But we'd always come home to the block to listen to Dirty's family.

Finally, one night Miss Cherry looked at me and said, "Come on, Buddha, let us hear *you* sing."

"Nah, I'm just gonna sit here and listen to you."

"Come on. Let's hear it. We know you love music. We know you sing when you're up in your room playing records."

I started singing and they were like, "Wow, we never knew you could sing like that." I think it made Dirty jealous.

Dirty's whole family can sing. Except Dirty. I always said Dirty couldn't sing but he could *sang*. Dirty sang loud and he sang with a lot of heart.

He sang with a warble that he played up on his records for comedic effect, but he couldn't compete with his mom and sisters, who sounded like trained singers. Dirty couldn't sing to match them, so he began to clown when he sang. He'd sing loud and operatic like Paul Robeson but throw in grunts and screeches like Screamin' Jay Hawkins. He threw in wails and hollers—the rapper Lord Digga called them Dirty's Indian war cries. "I rap, but I sing," Dirty told MTV News. "I don't know how to sing, but I like to sing." One reviewer said he sounded like a "dying hound," but Kanye West loved Dirty's sound: "His voice was unmatched," he said. "There was a time, when I was trying to get into hip-hop, when I would have cut off a piece of my finger to have his voice."

It never fazed Dirty that he couldn't sing. He loved to have an audience and he became an entertainer by learning how to get his family's attention with his own style of singing. I used to make fun of him. I would be walking by to go to the store and hear him singing in his house and I'd yell up to the window, "Nigga, you can't sing for shit. You need to hang it up. Hang. It. Up."

"Are you crazy?" Dirty yelled back down. "One day I'm gonna be an artist and everybody's gonna love the way I sing. I'm gonna mix it with rap."

"Yeah, right," I said. "That shit ain't gonna happen."

DIRTY WAS ALWAYS telling me I needed to meet his cousins Rakeem and Justice. Justice was a couple years older than us, so he'd take his little cousins with him to MC battles around New York. Dirty used to beatbox while Justice and Rakeem rhymed. The three of them formed a crew called FOI— Force of the Imperial Master. (FOI is also the acronym for Fruit of Islam, a defense/security unit within the Nation of Islam.) This was in 1985, when Dirty was seventeen. They passed around a tape of a song they did called "All in Together Now," and it became so popular that people started calling them the All in Together Now Crew. I wonder how many people who got passed that tape had any idea that they were listening to the earliest incarnation of one of the biggest hip-hop groups of all time. When they watched Rakeem, Justice, and Unique, they were watching the RZA, the GZA, and the Ol' Dirty Bastard from the soon to be world-famous Wu-Tang Clan.

GZA wrote most of the rhymes, but even looking back to those early days he gives Dirty credit as a performer: "He was one of the best beatboxers around. I used to write ODB's beats, write out the sounds on paper and orchestrate them. I'd hold my hands up like a conductor. We definitely had a bugged chemistry. We'd make up routines, battle other crews." They all used to have fun with each other—there's footage of an old talent show where you can see Dirty beatboxing while RZA does a verse that Dirty ended up recording years later for his song "Don't U Know" on *Return to the 36 Chambers.* We all used to DJ and rap and sing together, but we didn't know that this music thing was really going to happen for us.

GZA lived in Bed-Stuy, so he would come visit Dirty. GZA was two years older so he could travel around more freely to witness hip-hop around Brooklyn. He introduced Dirty to the music of early Brooklyn rap crews like Divine Force and the Mighty Mic Masters. RZA lived out in Staten Island, so when he came to visit Dirty he told us about the Force MDs, a rap crew from his neighborhood. Dr. Rock from the Force MDs let RZA borrow his Roland 707 drum machine, and RZA started to learn to make beats. GZA wrote most of the rhymes—he would travel around New York on the subway and buses and study the way rappers put words together. Dirty added the beatbox and singing and they had themselves a hip-hop crew.

Music wasn't the only thing RZA and GZA introduced Dirty to. RZA loved taking the train to Manhattan to see kung-fu flicks with his cousins in the old Times Square theaters—movies like *Five Deadly Venoms, Shaolin and Wu-Tang,* and *The 36th Chamber of Shaolin.* These films are where RZA, GZA, and Dirty picked up a lot of their slang, not to mention their eventual group name and album title. RZA started calling Staten Island Shaolin. Wu-Tang Clan called their first album *Enter the Wu-Tang (36 Chambers).* Dirty even took his name from a kung-fu movie called *Ol' Dirty and the Bastard.*

RZA and GZA also taught Dirty about the Nation of Gods and Earths, or the Five Percent Nation. The Five Percent started in Harlem in the 1960s as a splinter group from the Nation of Islam. Five Percenters divide the world's population into three categories: 10 percent of the people—the government leaders, the religious leaders—deceive the 85 percent and keep them from knowing the truth. The 85 percent are the deaf, dumb, and blind among us who buy into the lies the 10 percent spread, while the Five Percent are the poor righteous teachers, the niggas that see through to the truth. The Five Percent teaches that the black man is God and the black woman is the Earth. They teach their followers that Yakub—a black scientist—created white people to be a race of devils to deceive and keep down the black people, the gods. That's why you hear U-God say he's "makin devils cower" on Wu-Tang Clan's "Da Mystery of Chessboxin'," and RZA say he'll "snatch a devil up by the hair and cut his head off" on Dirty's song "Cuttin' Headz."

The Five Percent runs strong in hip-hop. It's the root of a lot of our slang. Niggas calling each other God—or shortening it to G—that's the Five Percent. The phrase "Word is bond" comes from the Five Percent. Even the term for MCs rhyming in a circle—the cipher—comes from the Five Percent. RZA has written that in many ways hip-hop *is* the Five Percent. You can hear the influence on Wu-Tang's rhymes if you know what to listen for. Listen to Method Man on Dirty's song "Raw Hide": "I fear for the eighty-five that don't got a clue." That's Five Percent teachings right there.

Yet the Five Percent teachings don't fit the lifestyle projected in a lot of hip-hop lyrics, including those from Dirty and Wu-Tang Clan. That's where Freedom Allah, Dirty's cousin, comes in. Freedom was almost ten years older than us, and he didn't approve of a lot of the things he saw on the block. And when he didn't approve of our behavior he wasn't shy about telling us. Wu-Tang Clan gave Freedom the name Popa Wu because he became our father without most of us having a real father. He was the group's mentor and spiritual advisor, an expert in the Five Percent philosophy, including the core mission that "each one teach one." He taught GZA, GZA taught RZA, and RZA taught Dirty. But Freedom—Popa Wu—was there to guide each of us. The Five Percent doesn't see anything inherently wrong with drinking, gambling, and drug use—so long as you don't get addicted—so Popa Wu didn't mind seeing us take a drink, but he didn't like to see us every day on the corner drinking and smoking and messing with girls. He wanted to see us act educated and civilized.

Even so, Miss Cherry was a Christian and she didn't like Freedom teaching Dirty a different doctrine. She didn't understand that what Popa Wu taught us is a way of life more than it's a religion. When Dirty joined the Five Percent Nation, he changed his name from Rusty to Unique Ason Allah and came home calling himself *God*. Miss Cherry said, "Rusty, there's only one God in this house and his name's Jesus Christ." I think Dirty was drawn to the Five Percent Nation because rather than hand him the Ten Commandments the way Christianity did, the Five Percent preached that there's no God in the sky and that each man is the sole controller of his universe. If you control your own universe you make your own rules, and that's what Dirty wanted to do.

I was raised Muslim, so I knew that traditional Islam doesn't approve of the Five Percent either—the Five Percent has its roots in Islam but rather than follow the teachings of the Koran, it encourages its members to study *all* the different religions and look for the basic truths that they have in common, but still realize that the true god is found within. I never got involved with the Five Percent to the extent Dirty did, but I learned a lot from its teachings just hanging around with Dirty, RZA, and GZA and listening to them talk about it and quiz each other on the 120 Lessons and the Supreme Mathematics. I learned enough that when one day Popa Wu approached me wearing his Universal Flag, real militant and real serious, and he greeted me by saying, "Peace, God, what's today's mathematics?" I recognized the sun, moon, star, and the number seven on the flag and I understood I had to show him I knew the Supreme Mathematics—the all-important numerology of the Nation of Gods and Earths. When a God asks you the day's mathematics, he expects you to show and prove, to demonstrate you know the Supreme Mathematics by parsing out the day's date. For example, if it's the third of the month, you'd start by telling him the number three corresponds to the concept of Understanding. So I told Freedom the day's mathematics and his face softened. "Okay, now I can talk to you, my brother. What's up? How you feeling?"

Talent ran in Dirty's family. We hung out on the corner with Dirty's cousins Sixty Second Assassin, Twelve O'Clock, Merdoc, and Shorty Shitstain. We would be standing outside rapping, singing, standing on the corner, hit up the Puerto Rican store on the corner for beers. One time

Shorty Shitstain sent us in to talk to the Spanish guy at the counter, get him to make us sandwiches while Shitty stuffed forty-ounce beers down his pant legs. He and three other guys got about six or seven forties and were back out on the corner rapping.

Shorty Shitstain is the beer master. He's been stealing beers since Putnam Avenue. From the corner store on Putnam to the great glorious bodegas of Los Angeles to Orlando's 7-Elevens, Shorty Shitstain is the master beer taker. That's all he wants is beer. We go into a store and he don't want no deodorant. He don't want no toothpaste. Nothing. None of that shit. One night me, Shitty, and Dirty were fantasizing about all the shit we'd buy once we got our record deal, and Shitty said to me, dead serious, "Yo, Buddha, when we get these motherfuckin' millions, don't even cut me a check. Pay me in *beer*."

On the block we didn't really have to worry about trouble because there was so much family. People would try to rob you on our block, but Dirty's older cousins watched over us to make sure nobody fucked with us. The only people that harassed us were the cops. Police would come by telling us to turn down our music. "Why they always want to fuck with us?" Dirty would ask me. "Niggas out here shooting and killing and we just listening to music. We ain't hurtin' nobody."

Dirty wasn't an angel. In 1987 and '88, when he was nineteen and twenty, he caught three charges for petit larceny, one for disorderly conduct, and one for resisting arrest. But the cops would roll up on us when we were just standing on our corner minding our own business. Dirty knew how to talk to the cops—he had a way of talking to people in general that would bring them around to his way of thinking. When he saw that shit was about to get crazy, he had a way of talking that would kill all that. You don't hear about Dirty being a peacekeeper, but Dirty could talk a nigga with a gun down in a second. The police was always harassing us, and Dirty knew how to talk to them to make them just walk away with their pride hurt.

One time the police rolled up on us, yelling for us to get down on the ground with our hands behind our heads, and Dirty just kept calm and said, "Listen, we ain't doin' nothin' but sittin' here on the corner just having fun, officer. We not on the corner robbin' nobody. We ain't trying to disrespect y'all. If you're going to give us a ticket for the beers in our hands you can do that. But throwing us on the sidewalk, telling us to get down on the ground like we some criminals, like we got guns in our pockets—I'll take my clothes off for you. You ain't even got to come close enough. I'll take *everything* off, cause I don't want to be down on no ground, man. And furthermore I didn't do nothin' for you to tell me to lay on the ground."

And the cops said, "All right, just put your hands on the car and let me search you and that'll be the end of it." They didn't find nothing, so they left us alone.

Out in L.A. cops was beating the shit out of niggas. It wasn't no news to us. Not if you lived where we did, and not if you listened to rap. It was 1989 when N.W.A released *Straight Outta Compton*, the album with "Fuck tha Police" on it. "Fuck tha police, comin straight from the underground/ Young nigga got it bad cause I'm brown." That took hip-hop to a whole other level of controversy. That song had the FBI and the Secret Service writing letters to their record company. But we heard that song three years before we saw the L.A. Police Department beating Rodney King on that videotape on the nightly news.

The way we grew up—the *place* where we grew up—it breeds a mistrust of the system. It's easy to think the world's out to get you when you growing up in a place where you see other people got so much and you got so little, where the cops seem like they're out to get you instead of protect and serve. The Nation of Gods and Earths has some compelling teachings for a kid growing up in that environment. They teach that the 10 percent of the people in control—the churches, the banks, the governments—are out to keep the rest of the world in ignorance. It made perfect sense to Dirty, a Brooklyn kid descended from Native Americans and African slaves.

I know we made ourselves easy targets for the cops. Dirty's cousins Twelve and Merdoc used to cry about it. "Why they always harassing us, man? Why they mess with us every time we come stand on the corner?"

"Hello?" I said. "You're standing on the corner with a forty in your hand. Don't you think they're gonna mess with you?"

"But it's mad motherfuckers out here. Why they gotta mess with us?

We just sittin' on the corner chillin'. Look at that nigga over there jay-walking!"

These things fuck with your mind: every time you try to have a good time, there's police lurking around the corner, waiting to harass you. Detectives walking around your block with their guns out, walking behind you, you start thinking the whole world is after you. All this affected Dirty. He knew how to talk his way out of a situation, but he also knew he had to watch his back in his own neighborhood.

I didn't cry about it like Twelve and Merdoc, but I felt the same sense of injustice they did. "I'm tired of this shit, too," I said. "Every night drinkin' on the corner, getting fucked with by the cops."

"Well, what do you want to do about it?" Dirty asked.

"Man, we got to work hard and do something to get up out of here."

Dirty just looked at me. "We are doing something, Buddha. I'm rhyming, you're singing and DJing."

"Yeah, but we're just doing it on the corner. I know we got talent, but we need a plan to get our music out there and make some money at it. We need to work at it like a business."

"Man," Dirty said. "All the music business wants to do is quiet a nigga down, dress him up and have him dancing and shit. I ain't with being told what to do. If I can't do it the way I want then fuck it."

CHAPTER 2

ENTER THE WU-TANG

Dirty and I took different routes to end up on the same stage. He traveled around New York City battling other rappers and performing at talent shows and open mics with RZA and GZA, while I devoted myself to spinning records as a party DJ. I've been working since I was thirteen years old. I was self-employed as a DJ for many years and I made my own money. I was living under my mother's roof, but I was supporting myself because she couldn't afford to support me. My part-time job at Burger King wasn't paying the bills, so I became a street pharmacist. Anything the streets needed I could provide, whether it was music or weed. I started out selling weed, spent some of that profit to buy better DJ equipment, and by the time I was seventeen I was traveling around with my equipment getting paid as a DJ. By the time I was twenty-two I was DJing parties, singing with an R&B group called Flamboyant, *and* selling weed.

DJing didn't pay all my bills, but still, I wasn't just no local DJ. I was throwing parties in Long Island, Staten Island, all over New Jersey, Philly, the Bronx, Harlem, Washington, D.C., and Maryland.

Somehow at a lot of parties—block parties, street parties, house parties, whatever—at some point the DJ's equipment always got shot the fuck up. But I kind of dodged all that. Any party I played never got shot up. I never had nothin' happen to my equipment. No fights broke out. I was lucky to avoid all that. Something about the music kept the peace.

I was a good DJ, no lying. I was making three or four hundred dollars a party, and people didn't mind paying it, either. They would recommend me to their friends and I'd give them the word-of-mouth discount. "You really need to get this dude." People would call me, "Yeah my people said to get a party with you," so I'd give them a little discount.

It was hard, though. At the beginning I did a lot of parties for nothing. Because I had to get everybody to know how hot I was, to get the buzz going. "I'll do this party for free, but next time, know you'll be paying."

I had all the new records. When Big Daddy Kane, Heavy D, Chubb Rock, or Run DMC put out a new record I was the first one to have it, before the record even hit the store. I would be record shopping like every three or four days. I was getting the two promo joints from the record store. At the time labels printed promos to be played in the store, but because I was a DJ and I bought so many records the guy who owned the store would give them to me before they came out. So at the parties I'd be playing the new joints before they even hit the radio. This was the late eighties and early nineties—this was before you could download songs from the Internet, so DJs made their reputations playing the hottest new joints before the other DJs got to them.

While I was DJing parties, Dirty was making his own moves. In 1991 we were twenty-two and twenty-three years old, and Dirty and I didn't see each other as much as when we were kids. I had my own things going on and so did he. I had my girl, Patricia, and we had a baby on the way. Dirty had settled down with his childhood sweetheart, Shaquita. They met when they were fifteen at a party at Linden Plaza. Dirty asked her to dance, and she turned him down. But Dirty was relentless and he ended up charming her.

Shaquita was a Brooklyn girl, born in Kings County Hospital in 1968, the same year Dirty was born. Her parents named her Icelene Purnell Barnes, but when she started dating Dirty and became his Earth, he gave her the name Shaquita. "In the Nation of Gods and Earths you have to have your own name," Shaquita says. "If you're a female, your God gives you your name. You have to have a righteous name, not what they consider a slave name. Dirty was good at making up names. He took it seriously. When he made up a name, he'd write out numbers from the Supreme Mathematics and attach letters to them to make up names. It meant a lot to him. If he gave you that name he meant it for you, and nobody else."

"Me and Unique used to race each other through the streets," Shaquita says. "We liked to race, and run, and jump double-dutch. He played skelly. He'd walk around with his boom box, battle other rappers. We were sixteen years old, running around, having a good old time. Unique's friend Sha-u-Born and his girlfriend Sabrina asked us to come with them to the clinic because they needed a pregnancy test. Sabrina asked me to get a test too, just for moral support. She wasn't pregnant, but I was. The next week my mother took me to Methodist Hospital in Park Slope, and we found out I'd lost the baby. Unique was crying. He was so broken up. I felt bad, too, but I told him, 'We ain't ready to have no baby. I got school and stuff. Nobody ain't got no money. We're too young.' He knew I was right, but he was still hurt. We took a walk through Park Slope together, dreaming that one day I would work in Methodist Hospital and we'd live in Park Slope. It was such a nice area to us. We really liked that hospital, too. We ended up having all three of our children there."

"In a way," Shaquita continued, "the miscarriage is what drove us deeper into our relationship. We had our first baby, Taniqua, in 1988, when we were nineteen years old. Dirty cheered for that baby with all his heart. When we brought her home he took her outside in front of our apartment at 112 Putnam Avenue and he held her up to the heavens, like Kunta Kinte's father did with his infant son on *Roots*—'Taniqua A'Shana Jones,' Unique shouted. 'Behold the only thing greater than yourself!' People were staring out their windows at him out there screaming in the moonlight with our baby. Dirty was a very good dad. When we were young, when there were no other alleged children involved, his life was our children."

In 1989, Barson Unique Jones was born. In 1991, Dirty and Shaquita had their third baby, Shaquita Nadasia Jones. Icelene came up with the name. "He hated that," she says, "because he wanted to name her. But he named Taniqua and he named Barson. I wanted to give her Shaquita. He was so upset about that, because that was the name he gave me, but he said, 'Fuck it, all right, if that's what you want we'll name her Shaquita.' He still insisted on coming up with her middle name." So their third child was named Shaquita Nadasia, and Icelene went back to Icelene. That's what she calls herself today, and that's what I'll call her from here on out.

To support Icelene and three kids, Dirty worked at a garage in Bed-Stuy and at a hotel in Manhattan, but with three babies he and Icelene just couldn't afford rent and food on what he was making. So around the time RZA and GZA released their first albums, Dirty moved with his wife and three kids into a homeless shelter in Brooklyn.

RZA and GZA both got record deals. I was hearing their songs on the radio, seeing their videos on MTV. "That's Rakeem and Justice!" I'd tell Patricia. "That's Dirty's cousins! I used to hang out with them on the block."

Dirty and Icelene got married on the advice of the shelter, to make it easier to place the whole family together. Dirty was working to get them out of there—working at the garage and the hotel but also rapping at talent shows at night and playing shows with RZA and GZA, trying to turn his music into a career. Dirty hadn't forgotten about music, and his cousins hadn't forgotten about him. GZA took Dirty and RZA with him onto a local New York City TV show called *Rhythm & Soul* when he was invited on to promote his album. Dirty talked a little bit in the interview and then he beatboxed while GZA rapped. Those early releases are by no means the best work RZA or GZA have done, but when I saw that TV performance I knew all three of them had a future.

GZA was signed to Cold Chillin' Records and RZA was signed to Tommy Boy. Word was that neither one of them was happy with their record labels because the labels wanted something radio-friendly and they weren't willing to go out on a limb for an unknown artist who wanted to try a new style. They wanted to put out pop rap and get a hit on the charts. People in Brooklyn laughed at RZA for his 1991 single "Oooh,

We Love You Rakeem." GZA's '91 single "Come Do Me" didn't get a much better reaction. The labels wanted to make them pop stars, and it just wasn't a good fit for them artistically. So behind the scenes the three cousins had come back together. RZA recruited six more of his favorite MCs, and they had formed the Wu-Tang Clan: the RZA, the GZA, Ghostface Killah, Inspectah Deck, Raekwon the Chef, U-God, Masta Killa, Method Man, and the Ol' Dirty Bastard.

Signing to Tommy Boy Records gave RZA access to Prince Paul, the legendary producer of albums like De La Soul's *3 Feet High and Rising,* which is one of the all-time classic records in terms of sampling. RZA has written, "When I first started producing, the only person I knew doing the kind of bugged-out sampling I was into was Prince Paul." Paul was known for having sampled everything from the Turtles to Johnny Cash to *Schoolhouse Rock* to a teach-yourself-French cassette, and RZA learned a lot from him about how to use sampling to weave the things that influence you into your hip-hop tracks to make them speak for your aesthetic and who you are. As RZA launched Wu-Tang Clan he was also in another group—the Gravediggaz—with Prince Paul, so RZA spent a lot of time with Paul in the studio. He used to bring GZA and Dirty with him to watch how Paul put tracks together. Paul says Dirty came off as humble and polite. The three cousins saw Paul as someone who had been able to make a career out of music without sacrificing the quirkiness that made him who he was.

Prince Paul would have his own artistic differences with Tommy Boy (as well as Def Jam and other labels) down the road, but from the beginning RZA and GZA felt held back by their record labels. They'd signed to labels at a moment when flashy, crossover pop rap was selling better than any rap records before, and the labels weren't willing to give them the artistic freedom people like Prince Paul had been given a few years earlier. RZA, GZA, and Dirty wanted Wu-Tang Clan to have a sound that people had never heard before. What people need to understand is that hip-hop is a form of creativity. Hip-hop shouldn't be controlled by anybody but you. It should flow out of you in whatever form it comes out. That's how Dirty approached it. He invented his own style of hip-hop. Dirty prided himself on being unique, and his uniqueness was the basis for the name that would make him famous: Ol' Dirty Bastard. Dirty explained it like this: "I'm Dirty because when I step to a mic I come uncut. I speak from the heart. The *ol'* comes from the fact that I was influenced by the old school—everybody from Al Green and Millie Jackson to the Sugarhill Gang." And Method Man explained the *bastard* part on the first Wu-Tang album: "There ain't no father to his style, and that's why he's the Ol' Dirty Bastard."

The name *Wu-Tang Clan* came from an old kung-fu movie about a Shaolin monk who set out to invent his own martial arts style. Wu-Tang Clan set out to bring something that hip-hop had never seen before, and just like Dirty had promised me back when we were kids on Putnam and Franklin, Dirty developed a rhyme style that mixed rapping and singing, and moved between shouting and slurring the words. He called it his drunken style. He was wild onstage and he was wild in the studio. People know Dirty as the most uncontrollable member of a group that was already untamed.

Dirty knew my rep as a DJ, and when he got his copy of that first Wu-Tang single, he brought the record to me. We hadn't seen each other in a while. I was busy with my music and he was busy with his. I was living on Franklin Avenue and Dirty happened to come down on Franklin. I had speakers that faced the windows at my crib, 441, and I had the speakers on and he could hear the music playing. I heard someone yelling from the street: "Yo, man! What up?" I look out the window and see him there looking up at me."Yo, where you been?" he asked. "I been trying to find you. I been looking for you for a long time."

I said, "Yo, G, I been DJing and doing shows all over. Where you been, Unique?"

"Word? Yo, that's crazy. Hold on. Let me go get something for you. I'll be right back." When he came back he had a box of Wu-Tang's first records with "After the Laughter Comes Tears" (aka "Tearz") on one side and "Protect Ya Neck" on the other. And that was the first time I heard Wu-Tang Clan.

Dirty put on the record and I heard "After the Laughter" first, because at the time somebody was pushing for that one to be the single. But Dirty said, "Yo, the song on the other side is my favorite."

And when I flipped it over and played "Protect Ya Neck" I was like, "Yo, this song is getting ready to go *off*."

"You really think so?" Dirty asked. "Yo, wait till you hear *my* verse!"

His voice came on. "Shame on you/When you step through to/The Ol' Dirty Bastard, straight from the Brooklyn Zoo."

He shrugged. "They callin' me Ol' Dirty Bastard now."

"Dawg, when people get hold of this they're going to go crazy," I said. "I'm going to start networking." I'd built a little network from a few things that I'd done with my music. I started getting the Wu-Tang record out to DJs at different clubs all through Brooklyn and Manhattan. I started getting it to the DJs in other cities and people out in Jersey. And Dirty started bringing me *boxes* of that single. I was playing it at every party, and a couple weeks later Funkmaster Flex started to play it on New York's Hot 97 radio station. Flex is one of the most legendary figures in hip-hop radio. In New York, still to this day, Funkmaster Flex is the guy who can stamp your record as a hit. If he drops those bombs on your record it's gonna take off. The single was creating such a buzz on the streets that radio DJs felt like they had to get their hands on it.

I like to think Flex wound up getting his hands on it at one of the parties I did, but either way, he got it. He played it. Next thing you know, about two weeks later, I'm hearing "Protect Ya Neck" on the radio and that's when everything started to happen. Everybody started talking about Wu-Tang Clan. And the part that they loved the most was Dirty's. I'd hear his voice singing "Baby, baby, come on. Baby, come on. Baby, come on," on the radio and I'd say, "Whoa, that's my boy right there." And everybody'd say, "Yeah, right. You don't know that nigga, man."

"Seriously. He comes to my house all the time. He's been with me since day one. He's like my brother. We grew up together."

"Word? You know Ol' Dirty Bastard?"

IT FELT GOOD to hang out with Dirty again. After he played me the Wu-Tang record he said, "Yo, what you doin' today?"

"I'm here chillin'."

"Come with me. I want you to meet the family." Dirty had saved enough to move them out of the shelter and into a little apartment in Bed-Stuy. I met his kids. I met Icelene. She was part of the Nation of Gods and Earths, like Dirty, and she carried herself very respectably. She wasn't into no wild shit, out late at night with other girls. She was a homebody, took care of the kids. Icelene wasn't a flashy, tight-clothes-wearing-type chick. She wore stuff that said *that's a new mom, she's respectable, she's well dressed.* She carried herself well.

Icelene made us dinner that night. Crazy whitefish, mashed potatoes, corn. And everybody's favorite—a big glass of cherry lemon Kool-Aid. Nice and sweet. If it didn't have a lot of sugar in it you wasn't drinking Kool-Aid. Dirty and Icelene put their kids to bed after dinner and then Dirty pulled out an Ensoniq ASR-10, a sampling keyboard RZA had given him. The ASR-10 revolutionized hip-hop production because it allowed producers to play a beat they'd made and sample a new sound over it during the playback. Dirty showed me how it worked. He recorded a drumbeat, played that back as a sample, then played a few notes on the keyboard on top of that. He was layering one sample with another, all with this one small instrument.

"Yo, tomorrow I want to take you to see RZA at the studio," Dirty said. "We thought *we* was makin' plans—wait till you see this nigga. He knows the business. He knows the producing. He's been teaching me how to make beats. Check this out."

Dirty played me a beat he'd been working on—the first beat that would end up on his album *Return to the 36 Chambers.* The song is called "The Stomp." Dirty sampled a few seconds of sound from the movie *A Rage in Harlem,* with Forest Whitaker and Robin Givens. I watched him run that sound through the ASR and loop it so that it repeated throughout the track. Dirty started to feel out the beat and rhyme over it:

> *Wu, gots like come on thru.*
> *Sooh! That's the call for the Wu.*

"Yo, that's nice," I said. "Gots like come on thru." Dirty freestyled a little more.

Shout out to my crew, tight as a belt, y'all.
Go by the name Big A from the shelter.

That was my first experience being there in person to see how a song started, watch someone tweak it and finish it over *years*, then the album finally comes out and people are driving by playing it.

CHAPTER 3

IN THE LAB

In the span of two and a half years, Dirty went from homeless to hood superhero, and I was there to see it all happen. He took me to see RZA at his place in the Stapleton Projects in Staten Island, and to Firehouse Studios in Manhattan, where he was working on Wu-Tang Clan's full-length debut, *Enter the Wu-Tang (36 Chambers)*. A lot of hip-hop producers refer to the studio as the lab, and watching RZA work I came to see why that was. The nigga was like a mad scientist, like Dr. Frankenstein bringing a new song to life by stitching together pieces of musical history. On "Wu-Tang Clan Ain't Nuthin ta Fuck Wit," RZA sampled drums from the Lafayette Afro Rock Band and Joe Tex, and a couple seconds of a vocal from the theme from the old television cartoon *Underdog*. You wouldn't even recognize that the sample came from the *Underdog* theme, because RZA slowed it down, cut it apart, and reassembled it into the sound you hear on the album.

RZA was bringing together the sounds and the styles that had influenced him growing up. Not only the records he listened to, but the cartoons he watched on TV and the movies he watched with his cousins. RZA didn't stop with digging through crates of old funk and soul records to find drumbeats and horns—he sampled dialogue and sound effects from the old kung-fu movies he and Dirty and GZA used to watch at the Forty-second Street theaters in Manhattan. The album is driven by sounds of karate chops and of swords being unsheathed and slicing through the air and clanging against each other. The first track, "Bring da Ruckus," opens with two swordsmen talking:

"Do you think your Wu-Tang sword can defeat me?"

"En garde. I'll let you try my Wu-Tang style."

Those samples gave the album a feel that said Wu-Tang Clan was ready for battle. You other rappers think you can test their skills, then bring it on.

Watching RZA in the studio I learned how to produce a record. Up to that point I was known for my DJing and singing, but working with RZA and Dirty in the studio, I became a hip-hop producer. I was making beats with the samplers and drum machines, mixing tracks at the boards. I found myself putting in so much time on Dirty's album that I neglected my own DJing and singing, but that apprenticeship in the studio was what helped shape me into a rap artist. First of all, I learned work ethic—I watched RZA work on the Wu-Tang Clan's album *Enter the Wu-Tang (36 Chambers)* at the same time he was working on songs for solo albums by Dirty, GZA, and Method Man.

Then I learned production techniques. I would watch RZA on the mixing board and realize that he would never put just two or three samples on a song. He would have so many tracks full of instruments that it was amazing. Most producers would be thinking they're only gonna have the drums—the kicks, the snare, the high-hat—and two or three melodies. Not RZA. He would have like twenty-five melodies on one track. On a lot of songs they did he would reuse the same beat but change the melodies. He's incredible for doing that. I'm telling you, I was so amazed by that. Instead of thinking of just getting one track done at a time, he would have five or six tracks working at once, off of one beat. He would take the same drums and change the samples and make six songs out of it.

RZA's production sounded like nothing people had ever heard—it was gritty and sparse but at the same time it was layered like a symphony. On "Shame on a Nigga" he sampled jazz piano from Thelonious Monk and overlaid it with funk horns from Syl Johnson. People criticize hip-hop for sampling because they think producers just steal an old record and rap over it—they don't understand that the piano may come from an old jazz record, the horns from a funk record, and it takes skill to combine those sounds into a new symphony. Plus, RZA played a lot of the piano himself. One of his signature sounds was a spooky piano clink he achieved by playing the notes on an actual piano-zither, then sampling them and looping them to repeat throughout the song. Running his piano through the sampler made it sometimes play back out of tune because the sampler's technology had not yet been perfected. But RZA took that shortcoming in the equipment and made the out-of-tune piano part of his sound. He brought string instruments into hip-hop and he offset them with hard drumbeats that weren't made for the dance floor or the radio because RZA wanted his music to sound aggressive to inspire his rappers to sound aggressive.

In 1992, the biggest hip-hop album in the U.S. was Dr. Dre's *The Chronic,* which was built around Dre's G-Funk sound, characterized by music that is slow, groovy, and melodic. Dre was sampling funk records while RZA was sampling jazz. I loved Dre's album, but it had California written all over it. Dre was making music for the people where he came from, L.A. *The Chronic* was music that they could drive around playing in their low-riders or have a cookout to—just the scenes you see in Dre's video for "Nuthin' but a 'G' Thang." But Wu-Tang was from New York, and RZA wanted to bring the sound back to New York with something up-tempo but gritty, with hard beats underneath jazz piano.

RZA's production was perfect for Dirty, but when Dirty would first hear a beat he had an ear for what was missing. One night I'd stayed at the studio longer than Dirty had, watching RZA work on a beat he wanted Dirty to rhyme over. Dirty called back a few hours later and said, "Yo, let me hear it." And over the phone the nigga could hear something that wasn't supposed to be in there and be like, "Yo, you hear that?"

"What are you talking about? I don't hear anything."

"Pull those levels down, one at a time. There. That's what I'm talking about."

"How the fuck you hear that through the *phone*?"

He said, "Pay attention, Buddha. Wake up. Open your ears." And that's how I got to be the perfectionist I am today with my music. Dirty said, "I want you to put everything you got into every track you make. I want every track to be the best one you ever did. RZA's the best, but I want you to strive to be better than RZA."

RZA and the Wu-Tang Clan changed the way hip-hop is made. From the way producers put tracks together, to the way MCs rhyme, all the way down to the way you sign a contract with a record label. Wu-Tang was a group of nine MCs who could each stand powerfully on their own, but when they come together to form Wu-Tang, watch out. Like that old cartoon, *Voltron,* where the robot lions come together to form one super-robot? That was how Wu-Tang worked.

When Wu-Tang signed to Loud Records/RCA in 1992, they negotiated an unprecedented deal—Wu-Tang Clan, as a group, would record for Loud, but the nine members were free to sign deals as solo artists with any record label they chose. Before Wu-Tang, when you signed to a label they owned you. If you wanted to go do a guest verse on somebody else's song you had to run it past your label first, and recording an album for another label was out of the question. RZA and GZA had both been signed to solo deals before Wu-Tang, so they'd seen the problems that come with signing a contract without negotiating to get what you want. What Wu-Tang did was shift the power from the record label to the group. They were like a hip-hop labor union. They had strength in numbers.

But to make this kind of power move in the industry, what Wu-Tang had to do was build a buzz around their name. They paid their dues playing mad shows all over New York and selling records out of the trunks of their cars. That "Protect Ya Neck" single they self-released caught the attention of the major labels. GZA's verse on that song even took a shot at the labels, almost daring the labels to sign them, saying Wu-Tang was too good for them: "The Wu is too slammin' for these Cold Killin' labels/ Some ain't had hits since I seen Aunt Mabel." But off that first single, when DJs started to play it, what I remember hearing most was them cutting Dirty's voice—"First things first, man, you fuckin' with the worst"—and playing his verse again and again.

Everybody in Wu-Tang loved Dirty. Everybody couldn't wait for Dirty to come through the door, because not only was Dirty talented, he was funny. He knew how to make niggas laugh when he came to the studio. He would get the work done, but he also knew how to keep you laughing. Everybody wanted to rap with Dirty, and Dirty wanted to rap with everybody. The fans loved him too—Dirty entranced the women, but he also was grimy, so he hooked the niggas too. The girls loved his swagger and what he was saying, but Dirty could say some dumb shit in the middle of a verse and niggas would say, "Yo, this nigga just went to the left on this song but he came back and it's still a killer!" Method Man even said it in an interview. They asked him what entertainers he looked up to and he said, "Yo, the greatest entertainer to me is Dirty."

Inspectah Deck agreed with Meth: "I remember the first time I met Ol' Dirty. RZA brought him over to his crib, and as soon as Dirty got there, he was like, 'Turn that beat on!' He was straight off the street with a forty in his hand, and he got on the mic and kicked some crazy shit. ODB was the same dude off the mic as he was on the mic. He never held anything back. He'd be in the mall, just performing, singing the theme to *The Love Boat*." Dirty mixed rapping with singing, but he did it in a way that was funny too. On "Shimmy Shimmy Ya" he sampled Richard Pryor's comedy album *That Nigger's Crazy*. Pryor had a joke about how the girls would turn him down—he mocks a girl's voice saying, "I ain't gonna fuck you, you can't even sing," then he tells the audience, "You have to *sang* or somethin' to get some pussy." That's how Dirty ended his song—"Shimmy Shimmy Ya" goes from Dirty crooning over RZA's piano tinkling, "Ooooh, baby, I like it raw. Ooooh, baby, I like it raaaaaw," to "I ain't gonna fuck you, you can't even sing."

Loud gave Wu-Tang Clan a $200,000 advance for their first album, which sounds like a lot of money until you divide it nine ways and take into account that RZA got a bigger cut than anyone else because he produced the entire album. Dirty walked away from the table with less than $20,000 in his pocket. Still, he was happy. He was making money from music, and this was only stage one of the plan. He knew his solo deal was in the works, and he trusted that RZA knew the business. Dirty was watching the way RZA handled his business and telling me, "We have to work hard the way RZA does. We got to get our own thing together, our own team, the way RZA did with Wu-Tang."

"What you mean?"

"All the niggas from the block. You're doing the producing. Merdoc raps. Raison raps, 12 O'Clock raps. Shorty Shitstain raps. That's our crew. Put us all together and that's the Brooklyn Zoo."

"That's what we should call the crew? The Brooklyn Zoo?"

"That's what Raison's been calling us. Yo, but we'll spell it with a U to make our Wu-Tang connection clear—you got the Wu, then you got the Zu. We'll put y'all on my album and springboard it from there. When the Ol' Dirty Bastard album comes out it'll let people know about the Brooklyn Zu before we start releasing Brooklyn Zu albums."

From the beginning, Dirty wanted to make our crew, the Brooklyn Zu, his own branch of the Wu-Tang Clan, just like Ghostface Killah had his Theodore Unit and Raekwon had his American Cream Team and Ice Water Inc. It's a rap dream to make it and bring your boys and your cousins and your cousins' boys with you. When a rapper hits it big he tends to start his own group or even his own label so that he can sign his people to record deals. Eminem has Shady Records, 50 Cent has G-Unit Records, and when RZA founded Wu-Tang Records the first acts he signed were Killarmy—which was RZA's brother 9th Prince's group—and Sunz of Man, which was his cousin Sixty Second Assassin's group.

Dirty had the Brooklyn Zu, which was me and four of Dirty's cousins: Merdoc, 12 O'Clock, Raison the Zu Keeper, and Shorty Shitstain. Then under the Brooklyn Zu umbrella we recruited Da Manchuz and the Zu Ninjaz, who were dudes we met on the road playing shows. Dirty loved the Zu Ninjaz: K-Blunt, Irie the Five-Foot Hyper Sniper, Obe, Hook Ninja, and Popa Chief. We first met them when Dirty and I started touring off his album and we did a show in Delaware at Cheney University. Popa Chief opened for us—he had a solo deal at the time. We went in, we performed, then we stood outside drinking beers with Popa Chief, Irie, and K-Blunt. Dirty liked them and he liked the way they rapped, so he said, "Y'all come to the hotel with us."

We hung out with them for two days, but Dirty had to go back to New York, so he told me, "Listen, I'm gonna give you like three or four stacks in your pocket. I want you to hang out here a few days. All them niggas rap, and they're nice on the mic. I want you to stay close to them. They'll be another chapter of the Brooklyn Zu. They're the Zu Ninjaz now." At the time they was the Five-Foot Ninjaz. Adding the Zu would tell people they were now part of Brooklyn Zu.

Dirty headed back to New York, and me and Blunt took a ride in the Suburban. I told him about Dirty's plan to bring him into the Brooklyn Zu family. "Yo, man," I said. "I have some shit to tell you. I see how everybody pay attention and the way you do things. I need you to get all of them together and let them know you the general and it's a life commitment, we gonna keep pushing no matter what." I told Blunt, "I got Da Manchuz. I want you to head up the Zu Ninjaz. They gotta follow you, Blunt, cause I can't tell everybody what to do. I need a general to handle that branch of the tree."

Even before Wu-Tang Clan's first album came out, me and Dirty were playing solo shows for Ol' Dirty Bastard and the Brooklyn Zu and making moves to establish our own team. That was all part of the plan. At the same time Wu-Tang Clan was recording its debut album, Dirty was in the studio with RZA working on solo tracks like "Cuttin' Headz." Method Man was working on solo tracks. GZA was working on tracks for his solo album. Everybody was watching RZA to learn how the production was done. RZA was the one overseeing the whole operation, but he was working on albums for Wu-Tang Clan, Method Man, GZA, Raekwon, himself, *and* Dirty, so some days he'd give Dirty a beat to rhyme over, and Dirty and I would record the vocals and mix the track and then play it back for RZA when he came back.

I started to understand Dirty's sound and the style he was looking for. I'd watched the way RZA used different compression settings for each of the Wu-Tang members' voices, and I'd developed a good ear for what worked for Dirty. Dirty would come in and lay some vocals, then I'd work on the mixing board to give his voice the character it needed and the track the effects it needed. The turning point for me, when I really started to feel like I knew what I was doing, was when RZA dropped off a new beat he wasn't completely happy with and said, "Something's missing in this one, Dirty, you know what I mean?" He played it for us and he and Dirty sat back trying to figure out what it still needed. Dirty turned to me and asked, "What you think, Buddha?" I gave them my opinion and they both nodded their heads and Dirty said, "Yo, son. That's my man. He's gonna be in the studio with me from now on. He knows what he's talking about. He knows what he's doin'. We're not recording without Buddha."

Dirty took me with him to the shows, too. I knew how to keep the party moving as a DJ, and I knew how to rock a show. Wu-Tang was playing concerts around New York. I'd help Dirty load up his Plymouth Sundance with cases of Olde English 800 and we'd hit the road. There were no hard drugs back then. Dirty loved to drink Olde English and he'd mess with weed when it was around—it was usually around—but he never liked to smoke too much because it made him paranoid. Wu-Tang Clan was selling tickets on the strength of the "Protect Ya Neck" single and word of mouth that they knew how to play a live show. Wu-Tang shows were known to be crazy. They were known to devolve into fights and riots because the Wu played the kind of music that made you want to stomp your feet and beat somebody's ass. I mean, shit, Wu-Tang had a song called "Bring da Ruckus." And the Brooklyn Zu, we was already labeled untamed niggas. What's the zoo? The zoo is a bunch of wild-ass animal niggas. You can't take your eye off them or they're gonna escape and run to center cage. The Clan would be ready to do the shows and when shit would jump off they were fightin' niggas with their fists, but the Zu would be the ones who would show up and people would say, "Oh, here come the flying chairs. Here come the pool sticks. Here come the broken windows." So when people left the show they were like, "That was the greatest show I ever saw. We got to see them perform *and* see people get they ass busted."

Dirty loved to perform, and he loved to see shit get wild. You've seen rock bands smashing guitars—Dirty was the hip-hop version of that. Even when he wasn't listed to perform he did it. When he was in the crowd at a show, he would jump onstage and snatch the mic. He'd snatch the mic from anyone. He didn't care. He did it to the Roots. He did it to the Lost Boyz. He did it to the legendary Doug E. Fresh. Dirty said it best himself: "I don't like to see wack-ass niggas doin' a show. If they not doin' it right, I'm gonna show 'em how it's done. I apologize for being like that, but that's me. It's something I'm trying to control." His mama didn't like it at all. "Rusty," she'd scold him, "that's not nice."

The Wu-Tang Clan made eight hundred dollars to play a show—that's eight hundred split nine ways. They pulled up to the venue in a beat-up van. After the shows me and Dirty used to steal the van from the rest of the group. Dirty would want to go home but they'd still want to keep going with the after-party. So Dirty would take the Wu-Tang van. Me, him, and the Brooklyn Zu would get on the highway and head back to Brooklyn. RZA and all them would be calling us: "Yo, bring the van back!" and Dirty would just keep driving, yelling into the phone, "Yo, I told y'all niggas I wanted to go home. Y'all thought I was joking. Fuck you. This is my van too. I paid for this shit too."

RZA says Dirty pulled a gun at one of those early Wu-Tang shows, at the Culture Club in Brooklyn. The fans had started to riot before the show even started—breaking windows and tearing apart the venue—so Dirty pulled a gun and started shooting at the ceiling. Now that's crowd control. This was all part of Wu-Tang's appeal. They were gritty. They were rough around the edges when there was too much cleaned-up pop rap on the radio. Hip-hop had gone through the pop rap explosion with MC Hammer and Vanilla Ice dancing in them shiny-ass pants, then Dr. Dre and Snoop Dogg blew up on the West Coast. Not to take nothin' away from Dre and Snoop, but Dre's production was clean and laid-back in every way RZA's was muddy and aggressive. You can hear it in the production on *Enter the Wu-Tang*. RZA wanted to keep the sound dark and muffled and dirty. He wanted to capture the feel of the hood in that sound, establish an atmosphere that felt like the places Wu-Tang came from. RZA and Ghostface were living in the Stapleton projects out in Staten Island. Method Man, Deck, and Raekwon were in Park Hill, otherwise known as Killa Hill. And you know about Dirty's block—we had family out there on Putnam and Franklin, but it was still a tough place to come from.

RZA was involved in a shooting in Steubenville, Ohio, not long before that album came out—he was facing eight years for attempted murder. Steubenville's a suburb of Pittsburgh. RZA and Dirty had family there, so they both spent some time there as kids. By 1992, RZA and Ghostface Killah had moved out there full time. RZA was dealing drugs, and in the course of the trouble that brought them from the Steubenville natives, Ghost got shot, their Steubenville friend Wise got murdered, and RZA got charged with attempted murder after a shootout with a rival crew. RZA's girlfriend was pregnant with his first child, and he was sitting in jail. He was in there thirty days awaiting his trial, and when he beat the case he rededicated himself to the Five Percent lessons and to his plan to make Wu-Tang Clan one of the biggest hip-hop groups of all time.

There were so many court cases going on with Wu-Tang while they were making that first album that they spent about as much time in court as they spent in the studio. Masta Killa and U-God were in jail during most of the time spent recording that first album. That's why you barely hear them on there. Masta Killa has one verse on "Da Mystery of Chessboxin'" and U-God has the first verse on that one and four lines on "Protect Ya Neck." Around the time of their first album, Masta Killa was best known as the dude who didn't like the illustrations that got published with a Wu-Tang interview in *Rap Pages,* so when he saw the reporter sitting in his car in a parking lot, he walked over and punched him in the face. In '92, Dirty was involved in a bar fight in New York and ended up getting charged with assault. He paid a $5,000 fine and was sentenced to five years' probation.

Almost all of the Wu's nine members had arrest records. I found my own trouble too. I went with Dirty and our man Pop for a Wu-Tang show out in Staten Island. Dirty had bought a little four-door with his advance for *Enter the Wu-Tang (36 Chambers)* and we were on our way to the show. Dirty said, "Yo, I wanna do something different for this show. I got to make sure my outfit looks better than anybody else's."

"Well, what you want to do?"

Dirty pulled the car over and ran into a little corner bodega. Me and Pop was like, What is this nigga doing? Dirty came out with a forty of

Olde E and a pair of stockings and hopped back in the car tearing open the packaging.

"You gonna put on some pantyhose, nigga? Ain't no girls out here."

He stretched the stockings over his face and tied up the legs on top of his head. Wu-Tang loved wearing those stocking masks. Inspectah Deck said, "There was a mystique about the group . . . I mean, we were wearing stocking caps on the [album] cover! We didn't care if people saw our faces. It wasn't a fashion show. Nobody knew us, but they knew *of* us. They knew the name. And that was powerful." I don't know why Dirty didn't wait till he got to the show to put the stocking cap on. We were on the main street by the projects and the cops drove by as soon as he stretched it over his head. They thought we was gonna rob the store. They turned on the siren and drove back around to us, hopped out with their guns pulled and screaming, "Get out of the car! Get down on the ground!"

I looked at Dirty. "I ain't getting on no fucking ground, man."

"I ain't getting down on no fucking ground either."

We held our hands out the window and Dirty yelled to the cops, "You know who we is, man?"

First they grabbed Pop out of the backseat. They threw him on the hood of the car and started searching him. Then they put guns in Dirty's face, threw him over the car. Then me. They didn't find nothing on any of us, but when they searched the car they found a gun.

I'm gonna tell the truth—it was Dirty's gun. It wasn't to hurt nobody. It was to keep us protected, because even though Dirty was getting paid a little more than a hundred dollars to play this show, niggas in the hood see him come off stage and they know he has money in his pocket. But before Dirty could speak my man Pop took the weight. "Whose gun is this?"

"Mine."

He got three years of house arrest with an ankle bracelet and three years' probation. Pop had actually never been in trouble, didn't have no record. So he took the weight for the gun.

If Dirty would have took the gun he could have wound up doing twenty years. He had a felony on his record from that bar fight.

It reminds me of the story I heard the Notorious B.I.G. tell in interviews: it was his gun but his boy took the weight because Biggie had more of an opportunity to make something of himself. It was the same situation with Pop and Dirty. "Yo, Dirty, when I get out and you're famous, don't forget about me."

They locked us up.

I was already on probation, and here I was caught in a car with a gun, so automatically I was staying without bail.

Dirty had a cousin who worked in the jail, so the police was asking Dirty where he wanted to go: general population or PC—protective custody. See, people in there knew who he was. He heard niggas calling his name.

"That's that nigga Dirty Bastard."

"Wu-Tang, nigga."

"Yeah, nigga, you in here now. All that rap shit, we gonna get some of this money from you now."

Dirty was screaming back: "Try me, motherfuckers. I really wish you motherfuckers would try me."

Then we're hearing even more taunts and threats and he sees it's going to be too many niggas against just one of him. "Yo, I want to talk to my cousin. I want to go to PC."

"Nah, fuck that, Dirty," I said. "I ain't going to no protective custody. I'm going to the population."

"I want PC."

"Fuck PC. I don't play that shit. Come with me, Dirty. I know everybody from the hood in there anyway. I know mad people."

I think Dirty knew that if he went to population with me he wouldn't come back out. They'd either kill him or he'd have to hurt somebody so bad to stay safe that he'd never see the light of day again. Everything would have been ruined. Wu-Tang, his own career, all that down the drain. "Nah, man, I need to be safe," he said. "I need to get out of here alive so I can get back to doing this music and getting this money and find a lawyer to get you up out of here quicker."

"All right, bet."

So we split up. He went to PC and they took me to population. The next morning RZA's brother Divine came and bailed Dirty out.

Pop got bailed out. I got arraigned. I was in jail for eight months. I didn't get no time off for good behavior because I was in there whoopin' ass. I missed my first shot at a record deal going to jail. I could have got signed. But the whole time I was in there Dirty was making sure that my commissary was fat. He would go check on Pop. He would go see Patricia to make sure she had money and everything while I was in.

During that eight months Dirty was still working on his solo album and working with Wu-Tang. This was just before the *Enter the Wu-Tang* album dropped. They were about to blow up. Loud reissued "Protect Ya Neck" as their first single—this time with "Method Man" as the B-side—and on November 9, 1993, Loud released *Enter the Wu-Tang (36 Chambers)*.

I came out of jail and the niggas was about to be famous.

CHAPTER 4

THE DRUNKEN MASTER

Eight months after I went in, Dirty picked me up in a limo. He took me clothes shopping. I got mad new gear and we went straight to a video shoot. The day I came out of jail, Wu-Tang was shooting three videos in one day: "Ain't Nuthin' ta Fuck Wit," "Method Man," and "C.R.E.A.M. (Cash Rules Everything Around Me)." It happened that fast. *Enter the Wu-Tang* reached No. 41 on the *Billboard* charts, No. 8 on the R&B/hip-hop charts, and went platinum. Not bad for a bunch of kids who used to stand around rhyming on Franklin Avenue.

But the place you come from has a way of following you wherever you go. Wu-Tang Clan was in San Francisco to play a show when they found out their album had gone gold. Method Man and Ghostface were headed to the bank to withdraw some money and celebrate when two police cars rolled up on them and pulled them over. Meth and Ghost were sitting there with a gold record, still holding their hands out the car windows to show the cops they didn't have guns. Ghost was in the passenger seat. He misunderstood the cop's directions and he went to open the door and step out of the vehicle. That was all the cops needed to snatch Ghost and Meth out of the vehicle, throw them facedown onto the pavement, and cuff them. All that just to take them to the station and release them, because what were they guilty of? But the worst news was still to come—only a few days later, back in Staten Island, U-God's two-year-old son, Dante, got shot in crossfire. The bullet passed through his kidney and hit his spine. The doctors were able to stop the bleeding and save his life, but he lost a kidney and the doctors said he'd never walk again. When I found out, I said, damn, ain't there any escaping this kind of life?

RZA had been shopping solo deals to the labels. Dirty, GZA, and Method Man were the first Wu-Tang members to sign. Dante Ross had reached out from Elektra Records to sign Dirty. Dante had been in the game for a long time. He was the A&R who'd signed Brand Nubian, KMD, and Leaders of the New School—which was Busta Rhymes's former group. He made his name by signing De La Soul when he was at Tommy Boy Records in the late eighties, and he'd met RZA back when RZA recorded for Tommy Boy. Now Dante had moved on to Elektra, and RZA and Dirty went up to his office there. Dante had heard Wu-Tang's "Protect Ya Neck" and knew the buzz around that record. He told RZA he wanted to sign ODB *and* Method Man and do a group with the two of them, but that didn't fit with RZA's plan for the Wu-Tang members to spread out across different labels. "Nah, that's not goin' down," he said. "Meth's signing to Def Jam. GZA's signing to Geffen. You get Dirty." So Dante signed Dirty. RZA had a plan, and there was no arguing with him.

Dirty would have been excited about signing to Def Jam, which was one of the first labels to be dedicated strictly to hip-hop. Def Jam was the home of LL Cool J and the Beastie Boys. But RZA's plan was for Wu-Tang to divide and conquer the record industry by signing solo deals with as many labels as possible so that each of those labels was pushing a Wu-Tang artist without putting another one on the back burner. Plus, RZA knew that Elektra was a good home for Dirty. Elektra had just appointed Sylvia Rhone chairman and CEO, which was unprecedented for a black woman. Sylvia is the most powerful black woman the music business has ever seen. Before she came to Elektra she used to manage En Vogue and MC Lyte. At Elektra she signed Dirty and Busta Rhymes and Missy Elliott. Then after Elektra she moved on to Motown and Universal Records and signed Erykah Badu, Stevie Wonder, and Lil Wayne. She helped make Cash Money Records a household name when they signed a distribution deal with Universal.

Once Dirty signed the Elektra contract, things started to get crazy busy. He was touring and recording with Wu-Tang, plus he had a commitment with Elektra to record an Ol' Dirty Bastard album. Me and RZA and Dirty started working in the studio to get his album together. My job consisted of making sure Dirty got to the studio and that he got the right kind of samplers, mics, and drum machines. Dirty was looking for a certain sound—I knew he wanted the studio with the Neve console. Other producers were using the SSL mixing board, but the SSL was a little more restrictive whereas the Neve board would let you play your trigger a little faster and have your drops where you wanted. That gave Dirty's vocals the character and the swagger that he was looking for.

We did thirty-day studio sessions, working all night splitting plates of Chinese food, drinking forties, making Kool-Aid with mad amounts of sugar. I had to eat in the studio because I damn near lived at the studio. I remember working all night and finally falling asleep in the studio on the ragged-ass couch, then Dirty came in and woke me up and said, "What's that sound I hear on the track?"

"Man, you fucking buggin'. I went and combed through this shit."

"Nah. I'm telling you, Buddha, there's a sound that ain't supposed to be in there."

"Nah."

"Watch." Dirty hit the solo button and there went the sound, a beep that had sneaked in.

"Yo, you heard that little beep through all that music? You're bugged out!"

After that I started going back in and trying to master that craft the way he had. I'd hear the Brooklyn Zu rap, I'd say "Go back in. Delete. You sound too happy on that one. The track is calling for you to be darker and serious. Not to a point that it sound like you gonna kill the world, but the track is asking for you to cry. Or it's asking for you to smile but not let them know that you're smiling. We gotta go back in." This was the craft that we needed to learn. We taught each other. Spending time with Dirty was like an education in rhyming. He and RZA and GZA grew up writing rhymes for each other and trading verses back and forth, just hanging out rapping, so when I started to get serious about writing my own rhymes, me and Dirty stuck with that formula.

We wrote rhymes while we were drinking. We wrote rhymes while we were smoking. We wrote rhymes while we were fucking. We wrote rhymes while we were in the car driving. One time Dirty picked me up in his car in Brooklyn. I was supposed to be home with my girl that night, chillin'—and I'd told him that—and two hours later we're getting on the highway. "Dirty, where the fuck we goin'?"

"We goin' to hang out with the Zu Ninjaz out in Jersey."

"What? I'm supposed to be home for dinner with Patricia."

"Ah, just tell her don't worry about it. Tell her to take the kids out to eat, 'cause we're gonna be gone for three or four days."

That's how it was. I never knew when this nigga was just gonna be ready to jump on the road. And if we didn't have clothes with us, he'd get on the phone to the label. "Yo, I need my check. Wire me some money." We'd get the cash and we'd go shopping. That way I couldn't use not having clothes as an excuse, because Dirty would say, "Don't worry about clothes. We'll get new clothes." And that's how it was. He would be in the car writing while I was driving, or he'd have a girl in the back, chillin' with her. Hitting the road like that relaxed him. "All right, what town next, Buddha? Let's go down south. Let's go to *Florida*!"

So we'd go away for a couple days and come back, then we'd be in the studio for two days getting out the songs we wrote on the road. We didn't know where or how we planned on putting those lyrics together, but we'd go to the studio and get them recorded. That was the way Dirty worked. Method Man couldn't believe how long he was taking. Dirty had signed his solo deal before Meth, but Meth was already finished with his first album, *Tical*. "Dirty was making his shit for damn near two years," Meth said. "His shit was taking long as fuck. If you listen to the album, there was so much time in between songs that the nigga repeated the same verse three times on the same album. Three times! That's proof right there that this nigga was working at a snail's pace." That was Dirty's process. He had fun making his album, and he took his time doing it. It couldn't have gone any other way or we just wouldn't have come out with the same album.

Method Man came to the studio frequently when we were working on Dirty's album. He'd listen to any beat RZA made and if he liked it he'd rhyme over it. He did a guest verse and the chorus on Dirty's song "Raw Hide." That was part of the Wu-Tang plan—the group splintered for solo albums, but the guest verses let you know Wu-Tang was still a tight unit. And Dirty made sure the Brooklyn Zu members got on his songs. He gave me a verse on "Snakes"—I got to close out the song. After Dirty, RZA, Killah Priest, and Masta Killa did their verses I came in and laid mine down. My rhyme style has changed a lot since then, but I'm still proud of that verse because it was the first one I did on an official, major-label release. In spring 1995 Dirty took me and Twelve O'Clock with him for his radio appearance on the legendary *Stretch Armstrong and Bobbito Show* on WKCR in New York. I got to rhyme a little bit on the air. Dirty was doing his best to promote me and the Brooklyn Zu and make sure we got some exposure on his album and his radio and TV appearances. He took me with him to his first appearance on *Yo! MTV Raps* and introduced me to the whole world. Ed Lover, the cohost, introduced Dirty, then turned straight to me and said, "Y'all better protect your neck 'cause we got one of the Wu-Tang in the house—my man Buddha Monk right here. He's got his own solo joint coming out, about to blow up the whole spot."

Dirty had been up all night with some girl, chillin', so he wasn't looking fully awake for this show. Ed Lover and his cohost Dr. Dre started talking to Dirty about his new album, then Dr. Dre asked, "Are you falling asleep on us, Dirty? What? You was in the studio all night?"

"Nah," Dirty said. "I was up all night drinking." I had to turn my head trying not to laugh in the camera. Then he launched into what people call his Drunken Freestyle: "Drunk as I can be, I am the Drunken Master . . ."

Dirty liked to call himself the Drunken Master, which was the name of one of his favorite kung-fu movies. Drinking was a big part of what made Dirty who he was in the studio. We drank because our families drank. When we were young our mothers used to give us a sip of their Miller or their Colt 45. We drank Colt 45 and Olde English 800. As we got older it became Private Stock and St. Ides. Dirty drank more than anybody. When he took it too far and got too fucked up, he'd shrug and laugh it off. He told *Vibe* magazine, "I got Indian in me, and you can't give an Indian alcohol. Once Dirty gets that shit in his system—that firewater—he's crazy." But we kept each other in check and looked out for each other.

You got some people when they drink they become violent. Me and Dirty never started no fights, but we'd tell a nigga the truth. To me that liquor was like a truth serum. One night Dirty and I were talking to niggas in the studio, all of us drinking and having a good time, and I said, "You know what, Dirty? I'm gonna tell you some shit I ain't never liked about you."

"Here we go, this nigga getting ready to start talkin'."

"Dirty, why does it seem like I'm working harder than you are on *your* album?"

"What you mean, Buddha?"

"I mean RZA gets credit for everything when I'm the one putting in work at the mixing boards all night. I mean, some of these songs you and RZA talked about on the phone but the hard work of mixing it and puttin' it together, that was *me*."

"You're gettin' credit. Your name's gonna be in the liner notes."

Dirty kept his promise—my name was included in the liner notes to *Return to the 36 Chambers*: "All songs mixed by the RZA, Buddha Monk, and Ol' Dirty Bastard." My name's in there, but not the way RZA's is. For one song—track fifteen, "Cuttin' Headz"—the liner notes read, "Produced by the RZA, Recording Engineer: The RZA," and I ain't even kidding, "Mixing Engineer: The RZA *featuring* the RZA."

Meanwhile I was the one calling ahead to get things set up at the studio, the one working to track down Dirty and make sure he came to the studio. Day in, day out, working and not being home with Patricia and my kids. While I was working, Dirty would go chill with his kids and Icelene, then once he'd gotten into the mode of chilling he didn't want to come back to the studio. Elektra treated Dirty like a star, but he missed just sittin' with his mother and being a kid to his moms, where she could braid his hair or just sit there, relax, and listen to music and have a beer. He wanted his time to be a family man. He didn't want to be running from this show to that show, no time for family. But the label would call Buddha Monk and say, "Yo, you gotta get him back in here." I did it because I knew it was right for his career, not because the industry wanted me to. I did it because I loved him. Because more than just being my brother he was one of the illest rappers. To be on-stage with him, working with him in the studio, you felt like you were working with talent.

Dirty ad-libbed a lot on *Return to the 36 Chambers,* like the intro to the album, the beginning of "Goin' Down," and the bonus track "Harlem World." He wasn't freestyle rhyming so much as just ad-libbing and talking, but he was saying some hilarious shit—talking on the intro about catching gonorrhea and how he was the greatest entertainer since James Brown. It's like Dirty was playing his own hype man. He sang on "Drunk Game (Sweet Sugar Pie)" and he overdubbed his own vocals, shouting out the R&B singers who'd influenced him. Improvisation was part of his style, but Dirty got distracted as easily as he got inspired. We'd be forty-five minutes into working on a track and he'd call a girl and say, "All right, well, I'm gone for the day, Buddha. You go ahead and finish doing what you got to do and holla at me later."

Dante Ross would come back with Dirty and say, "Let me hear what you got so far, Buddha." Dirty never had to worry as long as I was in the studio, but when he'd take off for two or three days I'd have to call him up and say, "All right, Dirty, listen, stop wasting time. We got to get in the studio and do this shit so that the world can find out who Ol' Dirty Bastard is."

"Okay, get in touch with Dante so he can get you a ride voucher to get there and get back home."

"Get there and get back home? Nigga, if I need a ride back home that must mean that you don't plan on coming to the studio. You just want *me* to go up there and work."

But I'd go to the studio anyway, because that was my job, and Dirty would call in to check in. He'd be down the block eating sushi, calling and asking me, "Yo, Buddha, how's my album going?" Sometimes he would drop by the studio to check in but then leave within fifteen minutes. Chris Gehringer, who was an engineer at Hit Factory recording studios, told *Vibe* magazine that one day when Wu-Tang was working on *Enter the Wu-Tang* in New York, Dirty said, "I'm going out to get a pack of cigarettes," and the Clan didn't hear from him again until the next day when he called from Los Angeles.

Somebody had to take charge. I'd learned to produce a record by watching RZA and Dirty in the studio, and I'd learned to rap by writing and rhyming with Dirty. The final part of my apprenticeship in the studio was learning to be a leader the way RZA led Wu-Tang Clan. So it became my job to get Dirty and the Brooklyn Zu into the studio and make sure things went the way they were supposed to go. It wasn't easy because plenty of the Brooklyn Zu members were Dirty's cousins and they knew they already had Wu-Tang approval. To them I was the new guy.

They were jealous when Dirty put me on songs, so they tried to get me out of the picture. I was focusing on trying to get Dirty to the point that he needed to be, and doing the shit that he needed to do, but some of the other niggas didn't like my ideas, so we argued a lot. "I can't do this forever," I said. "I can rap, I can produce, I can tour, but I can't fight with the team." The Wu-Tang Clan fought with each other, but nobody had it as bad as the Zu. Some of Dirty's cousins felt like he was valuing my opinion and was more focused on me than them, but I was putting in the long hours and the sleepless nights to make sure his album got done right, as opposed to everybody else just chillin' with him. They wanted to hang out with him and ride around in his car while I was the one putting in the work. We argued about how much time I was spending with Dirty and what they thought I was trying to get out of it for myself, as if I had my hands in his pockets.

When we recorded "Protect Ya Neck II the Zoo," Dirty's cousin Raison the Zu Keeper and I were in the studio arguing. Dirty left it all on his album. You can hear me at the beginning of the song screaming, "Fuck you." I said, "If he don't say nuttin', you don't say nuttin'. Nigga, fuck you." And that's how the song starts. You hear me yell at Raison and that's when Dirty starts talking, "I want to let all y'all motherfuckers know, whether you from Brooklyn, whether you from Manhattan, I don't give a fuck where you be, where you *reside* . . .

Sort ya stack out
This one's the blackout
357 to your mouth . . .

Then he said, "All right. My verse is done. Go, Buddha. It's your turn." And that's how he stopped the fight and told us to get back to work.

You have your team. You have your players. You'd see Busta Rhymes do a hundred different things but you knew his man Spliff Star was right there with him doin' it. Spliff has been Busta's hype man since the early nineties, but from the start Spliff was a rapper in his own right too. The problem with this industry is that the cameras are just focused on filming Busta Rhymes and not panning out to the whole team. They want superstars. But who's helping that scene come together? Same thing with Dirty. I'd bust my ass all night to get a song right and when we walk out the studio door who's getting all the fame? Dirty. He's getting all the star traction off that and nobody really realizes or asks, "How did you make this song? Who did you work with?"

That's the problem with the hip-hop game—the fans don't know what it takes to reach that level of stardom. They just see the stars as the geniuses. The only ones who really see the process that goes into making an album are the wives or the girlfriends or the girl that you bring to the studio and they see how it really goes down, what it takes to make the track. The people who are engineering and touching the buttons. Dirty would do his best, but when the camera starts to roll, you have only so much time to talk. If somebody calls you today and wants to interview you, you're not thinking of everybody you need to give credit to. Dirty would say, if I forgot somebody don't be mad. He thanked people in his liner notes but he apologized too: I know too many motherfuckers, he said. If I miss somebody in a shout-out, I'm sorry.

From the beginning Dirty told me, "Wherever I go, if I get on camera you'll be right there next to me." Dirty always made sure to introduce me to the reporters, to the people at the video shoots. Dirty would always say,

"This is Buddha Monk, this is my brother, he be doin' all the producing."
I remember somebody at the label damn near shut the door in my face,
thinking I was some hanger-on or something like that. Dirty looked the
man dead in the eye and told him, "Nah, don't ever judge him like that.
That's my producer. That's my artist. That's Buddha Monk."

CHAPTER 5

GHETTO SUPERSTAR

lektra gave us whatever we asked for. Dirty would sit around in the studio eating bananas and candy. We'd order breakfast, and no matter what kind of food they brought Dirty, no matter if they brought him omelettes, toast, butter, and everything, the first thing he'd say when he got in the studio was "I want a pack of Now and Laters." We'd have the table set up and the entire center of it would be candy. Dirty had his friends and his cousins in the studio with him sleeping on the couch, the Brooklyn Zu and the Zu Ninjaz stealing per diem vouchers from Elektra. We stole a whole book of vouchers from Rick Posada, the director of A&R at Elektra, and signed them with his name. And we wouldn't take the company car for an hour—we'd go out of state for a *week,* forge Rick Posada's signature, add a thirty-dollar bonus. Fuck it. We were tipping 'em with Elektra's money. We learned it from Dirty. "Lemme tell you how you really get on. Don't just give 'em the car receipt—put a hundred-dollar tip on there too."

"Come on, Dirty? A hundred dollars?"

"Nigga, I usually do THREE hundred."

And that's what we did, until Rick found out and Dirty called us real serious: "Yo, dawg, that's it. Stop it. No more vouchers." I had been using Elektra's car service to bring five or ten pounds of weed for me to sell in Albany, New York, with Patricia in the car pregnant, and giving the driver a hundred-dollar tip.

I ain't gonna lie. It wasn't just weed in the studio. There was plenty motherfuckin' cocaine. The first time I saw Dirty with cocaine we were chilling one night at his grandmother's house on Lewis Avenue in Brooklyn. We were writing rhymes in her spare room upstairs and when Dirty packed up to leave I saw something white in his bag. I didn't know what it was. It was new to me. I don't know where Dirty found it or how he got into it, but the next week we were at the studio and he had it again. I said, "Yo, that's what you had at Grandma's house the other day."

"Yeah, it's coke."

"Okay, word." And I wasn't a good boy. I had to try it. "Well, shit, nigga," I said. "I don't wanna be the nerd. Let me try a little bit with you." It wasn't good for me. I felt my heart race in a way that scared the hell out of me. I always stayed away from certain drugs. I was never an e-pill popper, never a shooter. I could never smoke crack in a glass. Stuff like that was just scary to me. Dirty never tried to force nothing on me or anyone else, but the power of seeing somebody feeling good and you're not feeling as good as them, that's worse than the motherfucker offering it to you. So I did my share.

Drugs came with the territory. Everybody in this industry has done drugs. As Wu-Tang got bigger and bigger there were more people around offering drugs, and the more Dirty was looking to blow off steam with drugs and women, and there was plenty of both. Between Wu-Tang's tour schedule and his own studio work, the scheduling started to mess with Dirty to the point that he wanted to take off months at a time and go enjoy the fun parts of being a rap star. "You can't do that, man," I told him. "You can't just disappear like that."

"I can do anything," he said. "I'm Ol' Dirty Bastard."

He'd try to ditch me, but I knew where to find him. I'd call our man K-Blunt in Jersey and say, "Listen, I know Dirty's there. I can hear the nigga breathing. Tell that nigga that if he don't get his ass on the phone I'm gonna bring my ass out there and fuck him up."

Finally Dirty would get on the phone and say, "What you want, Buddha? Man, what the fuck do you want?"

"Why did you leave New York? You got work to do back here in the studio."

"So?"

"So? What you mean *so*? You got me in the middle of this shit. I'm sitting here at the studio and people from Elektra keep coming in asking me where you are."

"Well, do your job."

"That's why I'm calling you, nigga. *You* got a job to do. I'm doing my fucking job. My fucking job is to get you here."

I saw the studio work as a job, even at the times I wasn't getting paid for it. Dirty felt different about it. Dirty was the one who introduced me to RZA and his five-year plan to take over the music business, but he just didn't share his cousin's work ethic. I mean, what was the Wu-Tang Clan's goal? There's an interview with Method Man and Raekwon included at the end of "Can It All Be So Simple?" on *Enter the Wu-Tang*. A reporter asks Rae and Meth, "What's your ultimate goal in this industry?"

"Domination, baby," Meth says. "We're trying to make a business out of this."

Rae says, "Longevity. Right now we still feel we ain't gotten what we want. Till we get the goal, we're gonna keep going."

I think if the reporter had asked Dirty his goal he might have said fun. Everybody in Wu-Tang wanted to make money to take care of their kids, and everybody in Wu-Tang wanted to make good music. But for Dirty, if he wasn't enjoying himself he didn't want to do it. So when Dirty showed up at the studio, he usually showed up with three or four girls—anybody from old girlfriends to groupies he'd met in front of the building.

I didn't really have time to be dealing with chicks too much. I had my girl at home. But there was so much sex going on in the studio. While three was getting fucked, six was standing at the board working. Three went out, three went in. But me, I needed Visine. I put in so many hours making those tracks sound like they needed to. K-Blunt put it in a rhyme. "While all of us is fucking, Buddha's making love to the ASR-10."

We had so many girls in the studio that sometimes I was the only one who had clothes on. Our mixing engineer Jack Hersca would head home before the rest of us, but Dirty told him to keep the mic on all night in case he felt the inspiration to rhyme or anything ill went down that he could use on his album. One night this crazy-ass girl named Denise went up to the mic and started rhyming:

> Destiny.
> You can't haaaaave me.
> You can't touch my fruits.
> It's the forbidden fruits.

The next morning we were working and heard that shit on the tape and didn't know what the fuck it was. Denise was long gone and it took us a few minutes to figure out who'd been on the mic. Dirty said, "Yo, Jack, did you tape something last night?"

I can't count all the women, baby mothers, and girlfriends that Dirty had. As far as Dirty's relationship, Icelene was a good wife. She stood by him. He didn't put it in her face. He didn't bring the other girls around. The other girls were content to just be with him and have his kid. It was the moment of ODB and everybody knew he was the shit. A lot of women wanted to be with Dirty. Not just hos and sluts, but women who really loved him. When he was in their town, they felt like their man was home. When he was home with Icelene, she felt like her man was home.

Dirty said he had thirteen kids. I know he had three with Icelene, and two with Suzie, and he had other baby mamas named Cheryl, Belinda, and Krishana. RZA said it first—"Dirty's downfall is gonna be women. He always wants to fuck and it gets him caught up in a lot of shit." Me and RZA sat and talked about it one day in the studio. RZA sat down one day and he broke it down for me. He said, "Buddha. I can tell you the whole future of the Wu-Tang Clan. Everybody's gonna do their thing and be successful, but I can tell you their downfalls too. A lot of the guys are gonna be jealous of each other and it's gonna cause a separation. Meth is gonna be doing movies. Meth's gonna be successful. Meth's gonna be all right. Me, people are gonna accept me and want me to do albums, but it's gonna happen later than it's gonna happen for Raekwon and Ghost. Everybody in this group is going to get a deal. And Dirty's downfall is gonna be women. He fucks with women too much."

It would seem more obvious to say that Dirty's downfall was drugs. But at that point drugs didn't control Dirty. Drugs made Dirty feel like fuckin'. On tour, Dirty would get high at the hotel and call three different bitches to see which bitch was available to come to the hotel for the night. He would call Number One, tell her to get dressed. Call Number Two, tell her to get dressed. Call Number Three, tell her to get dressed. Two of them would call back and say they couldn't make it, couldn't get someone to watch their kids or they had to stay home and watch their little sister and brother.

So, boom, he would take the one that showed up.

I said, "Yo, how does that work? What if they *all* wanna come to the hotel?"

He said, "That's easy. You give 'em two hours apiece and send 'em home. The last one you keep overnight."

"All right," I said. "That's what's up."

I think Dirty loved every girl he ever dealt with. I think he couldn't find what he wanted in just one girl. Not even Icelene. Icelene was the one, but Dirty still wanted *another* one. He wanted something beyond her. He wanted something that would be almost as good as Icelene but he couldn't find it in one package, so he made him a package of fifteen girls to become that one girl. There was Belinda in Jersey City—she was so sweet and she wasn't no stress for Dirty. He loved going and picking her up and spending time with her. She had a car and a good job and all that. She wasn't with Dirty for the money. She was crazy for him. She was quiet. She had beautiful creamy skin and a terrific body. She would dress up nice and look respectable. Then there was Passion, who was a little tough on Dirty because she knew there was a whole lot of bitches that wanted him. When they got together they had their fights and arguments but Dirty loved the shit out of her.

All the girls met Dirty's mother. All of them loved Miss Cherry. All the girls respected me. They loved me. Dirty didn't like a lot of the fam around his girls, because he tended to get suspicious. He would say stupid shit like, "Yo, you fuck my girl?" And niggas would get offended. He tried it one time with me and I said, "This conversation is over, nigga. I would never fuck your girl. Don't come to me with that shit about fucking your girl. They use me to get a message to you." I'd be walking down the street or driving in my Suburban, and my phone was ringing, the girls was calling me. Some of them still call me.

They'd call and ask me where Dirty was at, and as soon as I'd get off the phone, Dirty'd be asking, "Who was that calling? Why is she calling you?"

"'Cause I know where to find *you*."

"Yeah, you right. Well, what did the bitch say?"

"Look, man, you call her. I ain't getting involved."

They all were beautiful women. I can't say nothing bad about any of them. They all had a part to play in Dirty's life in making him who he was. They all knew about each other—that's the fucked-up part of it. They all knew about Icelene, too. I felt bad when I first met them because I didn't know if they knew Dirty was married. It kind of put me in a bad position because Icelene was a good sister to me, but also I respected them. Then they'd start talkin' about her, so I knew they knew. If they was fucking him they knew that he had Icelene. If they wanted to be a part of it, they understood their role. The girls that was talking to Dirty wasn't talking to him because he had money. They was talking to him because he had knowledge and wisdom. When Dirty was with a girl in his car he would play the Temptations, the Chi-Lites, the Manhattans. Everybody else was riding around bumping Ol' Dirty Bastard, but when the women got into Dirty's car he would mesmerize them with some Marvin Gaye.

They were all my sisters. They were truly incredible. I don't know if they know this, or if they've ever heard it anywhere else, but I just want to thank them for everything they did to make my brother who he was. Each one of them gave him a part of them that made him who he was. He's stressed out about this, he's stressed out about that. He's gonna chill in Manhattan and get away from everybody for a minute 'cause he has a girl in Manhattan. Then it's "Oh, you think you know where I stay? Well, now I got a new girl in Jersey. Buddha, don't tell nobody."

Meanwhile Dirty didn't like Icelene to be around his friends. He'd stay up all night drinking with some random girl, but he didn't trust anyone around Icelene. "Unique didn't like me being around other people," she told me. "I was not allowed to be around anybody because Unique didn't trust *any*body." It blew up when me and Dirty brought our girls on tour in Europe with us. He and Icelene left their kids with her mom and I left my daughter with my mother so that Patricia could come along. It was the four of us. Our girls had put up with us spending our nights in the studio or driving all over the country, so we treated them to a European vacation. We went to Germany and London together.

Me and Dirty went out to do the London show while Patricia and Icelene stayed at the hotel. "We was having such a good time talking over dinner," Icelene remembers. "We even went swimming together. It was me and Patricia really getting to know each other. We'd been friends for a while, but this was different because it was just me and my friend. I liked being around another female. It felt good. Dirty didn't like me around people to the point that he didn't even like me around his family. I was totally isolated. So hanging out with a friend was a rare thing for me."

Me and Dirty finished the show and came back to the hotel. Icelene went back to her and Dirty's room to lie down and Patricia pulled me aside and told me something. Looking back I should have been more suspicious, but at the time I felt like I had to tell Dirty. He was my friend and I felt like I was looking out for him. "Dirty was angry," Icelene remembers. "He confronted me back in our room—'Patricia told Buddha some shit.' I had no idea what he was talking about. What the hell could Patricia have possibly said? We'd had a good time together. Dirty marched me—damn near pushed me—down the hallway to Buddha and Patricia's room. Buddha opened the door and Patricia didn't look at me. She looked at Buddha. Buddha said, 'Tell him. Tell Dirty what Icelene said.' Patricia looked at Buddha Monk and said, 'She said she don't want to be with him anymore.' She lied on me. I never said that."

The next morning we went downstairs to the lobby to check out, and Icelene wasn't speaking to anyone. Dirty was angry with Icelene. Icelene was angry with Patricia. I was angry with Icelene for what I believed she'd said, and for her trying to call Patricia a liar. It was a tense breakfast. "I had shades on," Icelene remembers. "I was so embarrassed I didn't want to look at nobody. They'd seen my husband pull me down the hallway."

Dirty was angry with me for a minute—guilt by association—but he got over it soon enough. There was tension within the couples, and now there was tension between them. Icelene hugged Patricia and they made up, but that was the last time we all went on tour together.

ICELENE CAME TO the studio when we recorded "Goin' Down," the song that opens with Dirty making that croaking sound. RZA had already let Dirty hear the beat and Dirty just went in the track when we got the reel. We put it on, Jack Hersca pulled everything up, and Dirty just started pulling shit down like, "Jack, cut the faders in and all that. I want them to have action in it and I'm gonna start premixing how I want the beat to start and everything." Dirty just started messing with the faders, bringing one of them up for a minute then turning it back down. And when he got it put together the way he wanted he would just sit there and listen to the track again and again for like twenty minutes. Just listen. And then he'd say, "Yo, Jack, take me from the beginning, before the music starts."

And that's when he started making that croaking sound with his throat. "AAAAAAAAHH. Yo, remember when we was young and we used to see who could do this the longest?"

And I'm thinking, Oh, this nigga is fuckin' buggin'. What the fuck is he doing?

Then Dirty revealed his idea to have Icelene yell at him about groupies and put it on his song. Dirty remembered that moment from their lives, so he called in Icelene to re-create it. "Fuck that bullshit, Unique. You my motherfuckin' husband. I ain't got no fuckin' time for these bitches callin' my motherfuckin' house. You got three fuckin' babies to take care of. Fuck this shit." And Dirty starts singing "Over the Rainbow" to drown her out.

That's what made Dirty ill. It wasn't only his music. The ill shit that he talked about in his music, he did it in person for people to see. It wasn't just album talk. He lived that shit. After Dirty was selling gold and platinum he would get his old tapes and put them in the BMW and just blast it driving through the hood to get a forty from the corner store and stand on the corner drinking. People would see it was Ol' Dirty Bastard and do a double take: "Nigga, you makin' so much money. Why you still goin' in the store stealin' forties?"

Dirty wanted to share the wealth with his people in Brooklyn. He wanted the people who came from where he came from to share in his success. There was never a minute that Dirty wasn't concerned about his people and his community. Dirty would hit up the Brooklyn businesses. When he needed that certain skullcap for a show, or he needed gloves or funny glasses for a video shoot, he'd go to the little shops owned by Indians, Africans, or Spanish people and he'd buy up all they had. He didn't go to the major stores. He liked them little bodega stores where everybody else shopped.

If you was in Brooklyn and he was in Brooklyn, if you were standing in line at the bodega and you were two dollars short, Dirty would give you two dollars. I remember standing in line behind this woman—the cashier was frowning and she was asking, "How much am I short? Can you take something out?"

And Dirty said, "Nah, don't take nothing out—give her all that and some extra pies and cakes, whatever she needs. I'll pay for it."

"Thank you so much, mister."

"You don't have to call me mister. My name is Ol' Dirty Bastard."

"Oh my God, Ol' Dirty from Wu-Tang Clan? Oh my God, thank you so much."

Popa Wu said he seen Dirty park his car at a stoplight and jump out and give money to all the kids on the corner. Police told him to move his car but he didn't stop till he gave some to everyone. That was who Russell Jones was. You know why they loved Dirty so much in the hood? Because he didn't just act hood on television. You'd see him out there all the time, hear people talk about seeing him. "Yo, I was just watching Ol' Dirty Bastard on TV, and that nigga drove right by here. He just went to the fish market right off Brooklyn and Fulton Street."

He was in Wu-Tang Clan but he didn't want to be a rap star and not be human. He wanted to be in the public and talk to people like a normal person. One day we walked into the fish market and he said, "Yo, before y'all even start asking me, I ain't takin' no fucking pictures. Don't even ask me about music. Let's talk about life!" Everybody in the room knew this nigga wasn't on that star shit. But once people started talking to him he would get comfortable. It was a lesson for him and a lesson for all of us. He'd listen to them and they'd listen to him.

"Where you buy your clothes at, Dirty? Where you shop?"

"I don't go for none of that fancy shit. Motherfucker, I'm from the fucking hood. I shop where you shop!"

"Dirty, where's your diamond watch?"

So as opposed to them seeing their favorite rapper on TV with a diamond watch that they couldn't afford themselves, he wanted to let people know the truth. "Nigga, I got one of those in my dresser drawer. Same watch you got on. Matter of fact, I've been looking for that shit. I'm gonna go home and find it and put it on." He would inspire people. "Yo, I rock the same shit you rock. Don't you see my pants is turned inside out? I keep the pockets out so nobody can't pickpocket me."

He was still a hood-ass dude. He didn't make people think he was walking around with ten thousand dollars in his pocket. When he came to the fish market he wanted to talk to people as a human being, and that's how he got people to talk to him.

"Dirty, what kind of fish you like?"

And before he went out the door, Dirty had taken pictures with all of them.

THE DANGEROUS SIDE to Dirty wanting to stay in the hood was that dudes in the hood knew who Dirty was and they knew he had money.

One night Dirty noticed a car following him, real slow. He was walking home by himself, so he started to get paranoid. He turned a couple corners and the car was still there, still creeping along behind him. He didn't know who these dudes in the car was or what they might want. He just knew he needed to get the fuck off the street before something went down.

So he ducked into someone's yard, and wouldn't you know they had three rottweilers back there? So the dogs is barking and snarling at him, the car's still creeping through the alleyway, and Dirty gets down on his hands and knees and crawls into this woman's house through the doggy door. "Somebody's after me! Call the cops!"

The woman dialed 911 but the whole time she's talking to the dispatcher, Dirty's got these three giant rottweilers coming after him. The dogs chased him upstairs and he finally got so scared of them that he jumped out a second-floor window and ran off down the street. The cops picked him up a few blocks away. They didn't want to listen about nobody following him. They said he was on drugs and paranoid.

But it was like that Nirvana song that was out at the time said, "Just because you're paranoid don't mean they're not after you." It wasn't twelve hours later when Dirty got shot. Nobody's sure exactly how it went down. The newspapers called it a dispute over music with some rival rappers. There was another crew called Brooklyn Zoo Together Forever that people said Dirty had been talking to earlier that day, so people say they set him up over us calling our crew Brooklyn Zu—but I don't know if that's really the case. I think it's more some niggas were tryin' to rob him. Period. Because they knew who he was and they knew he had money.

Dirty was on Kingston in Bed-Stuy. He was headed to see his girl over there named Kia. Some niggas tried to grab him up and rob him. He wouldn't give up what they wanted and one of the niggas shot him, right there on the street. He jumped in the car and drove straight to the hospital. To fans, Dirty's having been shot came to speak for the recklessness that was so much part of his image, but really he was the victim of some niggas robbin' rappers for money, because apparently, the same people were planning on robbing Q-Tip from A Tribe Called Quest. I was talking to another girl I knew over in Bed-Stuy, and she said the rumor was Q-Tip was about to get robbed.

Dirty called the Sound Factory, where we knew Tip was recording, and we went into the vocal booth and turned the mics off. I said, "Tip, I heard you getting ready to go on Kingston? I heard you're talking to a girl over there."

"Yeah?"

"Well, don't go over there, 'cause niggas is trying to set you up."

"Word, Buddha?"

"Don't go over there. Because niggas is waiting for you to come through the block and rob you."

Niggas was robbing rappers. They robbed Busta Rhymes. They robbed Foxy Brown. Like Greg Nice of Nice & Smooth said, "Stick-up kids is out to tax," meaning that when thieves see a rap star making money on MTV shouting out the name of their hood, they're liable to come after some of that money. A nigga shot Dirty in Brooklyn, and just two weeks later some niggas shot Tupac Shakur in Times Square. Pac was heading into Quad Studio to record when it happened—he was in the lobby on his way onto the elevator. Niggas told him to give up his jewelry and when he wouldn't do it they shot him five times. Pac's shooting kicked off the whole East Coast vs. West Coast wars in hip-hop because Pac was convinced that Bad Boy Records had set him up. Pac was shot in the lobby and Bad Boy's Notorious B.I.G. and Puff Daddy were recording just a few floors above him when it happened. Pac was signed to Death Row Records out in L.A., so it became an East Coast vs. West Coast thing. Pac accused Bad Boy in an interview, then Pac and Biggie wrote diss songs back and forth taking verbal shots at each other.

For the most part, Wu-Tang Clan stayed out of the whole East–West rivalry. They represented New York, but the Clan was a phenomenon in itself. They was cool with people on either coast. Dirty said it on "The Stomp": "I admire true niggas like Dre and Snoop." Wu-Tang's Masta Killa even sampled Tupac saying in an interview that he loved Wu-Tang and would love to work with them. Dirty wasn't involved in a war of words with any other rapper. Ghostface and Raekwon from Wu-Tang didn't like Notorious B.I.G. calling himself the king of New York, but Dirty didn't take part in that East Coast–West Coast fight. He told *Billboard* magazine, "I wouldn't say my shit is New York. I wouldn't say it's West Coast. I'd just say it's Ol' Dirty." When they asked him are you East Coast or West Coast he said, "I'm all coasts."

Tupac set off the whole East–West conflict when he became convinced that Biggie and Puff Daddy were behind his shooting, thinking some niggas he'd been friends with had put out a hit on him. Then he went on record and accused them of having had something to do with it, and they got pissed off about being accused. Niggas were blaming and threatening each other in interviews and on songs back and forth. And the public was loving it, just buying it up. Pac's lyrics became more focused on his mortality to the extent that some fans believe Pac prophesied his own death, but the nigga just saw it coming. When you got niggas gunning for you like that, you know it's just a matter of time.

After Pac got shot at Quad, Dirty started locking down his own studio at Quad so tight that the owners would have to come to us personally and ask if it was okay for somebody to come in. People couldn't get upstairs unless Dirty personally let them upstairs. Getting shot will make a man paranoid. If somebody shoots you and the nigga's dead or behind bars, it's one thing. But when nobody knows who did it—and the cops don't want to investigate—that will make a nigga watch his back.

CHAPTER 6

PUPPERIZED

irty moved out of Brooklyn with Icelene and the kids to try living in the suburbs. He rented them an apartment in Harrisburg, Pennsylvania, but as much as he wanted the change in lifestyle to work for his family, it just didn't work for him. "Niggas don't even listen to hip-hop out here," he complained. Brooklyn was in him. That's where his people came from. He started making trips back and forth, leaving Icelene fifty dollars to feed the kids for the week.

Dirty came back to Brooklyn to speak to his mama and sit down to have a powwow with Popa Wu, who was a stabilizing influence for the entire Wu-Tang Clan. When the Wu went into battle and came home with cuts and bruises, Popa Wu patched them up and repaired them and got them ready for the next battle. When everybody started getting discouraged or sidetracked, he would sit and chill with them and help them get back on track. That was Popa Wu.

That was Popa Wu for Dirty. That was Popa Wu for me. That was Popa Wu for all of the Wu-Tang members. But we wouldn't only go see him when we were down or discouraged. We would sit down with him and sing and drink and play chess and talk about life and how we wanted to do music and where we wanted to go with it. He was our father, he was our teacher. "I didn't teach you go out there and fuck groupies," he told Dirty. "I taught you how to respect a woman, taught you how to put knowledge into your rhymes. You've been given a platform to speak to the people. You can educate these people instead of destroy their dreams. Your duty as a civilized person is to teach the uncivilized. So what happens if you're acting uncivilized, God? That is not the way. If you're comin' in the name of the Nation of Gods and Earths, you shouldn't be doing that. I'm here to tell you that is wrong."

The next morning Dirty called me and said, "Buddha, what you doing?"

"I'm about to head to the studio."

"Drop all that. We're going to pick up the kids and go out. We're taking a daddy day. The album can wait."

I couldn't believe how much Dirty's kids had grown. Taniqua was six years old, Barson was five, and his youngest daughter, Shaquita, was three. Dirty picked up his kids, I picked up mine, and we took them to Coney Island. Dirty loved Coney Island. He loved eating fried oysters and clams and shrimp. He loved taking the kids on rides and watching them have fun. He was like a big kid himself, but he still took time to talk to his kids about what was important. "Are you doing good in school?" he asked Barson. "How many little girlfriends you got over there?"

Dirty was trying to take a day off and get his priorities straight, but everywhere we went that day people would run up to Dirty and yell, "ODB! ODB!" and he'd say, "Yo, man, I'm chillin' with my family today, kid. I'm not signing no autographs. I'm not Ol' Dirty Bastard today. I'm Russell Jones right now. I'm just a regular human being like everybody else, trying to let my kids enjoy themselves." He didn't want anybody to impose on that. People would still beg, like "Can I get just one picture with you?"

"I just told you. This is my kids' time."

He wanted to stay longer but people kept hounding him for autographs. We didn't even get to ride the Cyclone.

Dirty was starting to feel trapped by his success. He wanted to be able to take his kids to Coney Island. He wanted to walk down the street in the hood and not have somebody point at him. He wanted to hang out with the people and feel free. Plus, he was starting to feel restricted by his record label, and GZA and RZA had warned him to beware of that.

Dirty came up with the term *pupperize*: "Yo, Buddha. Elektra wants me to do this public service announcement at the front of my single. Man, the record industry be tryin' to pupperize me."

"What the fuck you mean, pupperize?"

"You know, man, *pupperize*. Turn me into a puppet." That was his Ebonics for the day.

Dirty didn't like the way Elektra had approached him with the request. The younger dudes at the labels knew how to talk to Dirty. Dirty never gave Dante Ross a problem. Whatever Dante Ross wanted, Dirty would do it. But when Sylvia Rhone or the higher-ups from Elektra came in the building, shit would start going wrong for Dirty. "Y'all ain't respecting me as an artist," he'd tell them. "We sitting here trying to make shit happen, trying to get shit poppin', then y'all are telling us we got to take a bunch of time off and clear this sample and clear that sample and make sure we can make the song radio-friendly. You know what? I don't want to do it no more. Y'all killed the inspiration."

Elektra wanted him to change the chorus of the second single, "Shimmy Shimmy Ya," where he said, "Ooh, baby, I like it raw." They knew he was talking about having unprotected sex—and this was at the height of the AIDS awareness era, so they knew the radio stations weren't going to play Dirty's single. Dirty said he wasn't changing shit, but in the end he was willing to compromise and offset his lyrics with a public service announcement the label had him record and send to the radio stations to play before the song: "Yo, this is the ODB. Trying to tell everybody right now, protect your neck while protecting yourself. Wear a condom, 'cause the only thing I like raw is my music." Then it'd kick right into "Ooh, baby, I like it raw." That was the only way that his song would make the charts. All Dirty had to do was say he was talking about music when everybody knew he was talking about pussy.

Dirty's album came out in March 1995, when hip-hop was bigger than ever before. Tupac's album *Me Against the World* debuted at No. 1

on the *Billboard* 200. Two weeks later, Dirty's *Return to the 36 Chambers: The Dirty Version* sold 80,000 copies its first week. He got four stars in *Rolling Stone*—they called him the most original vocalist in hip-hop history. Elektra threw Dirty an album-release party in New York, but Dirty was having his own party back in the hotel room. The label brought in Pete Rock to DJ and MC Supernatural to open the show before Dirty was supposed to hit the stage. Supernatural was a freestyle rhyme champion—he was known for making up his rhymes on the spot. He pointed at a painting on the wall and brought it right into his rhyme. He was imitating the voices of other rappers, rappin' like he was Biggie and DMX. He played a long set that night, but when he finished there was still no sign of Dirty.

The whole time Dirty had been at the hotel and didn't want to leave to go to his own album-release party. Some of the Brooklyn Zu and me finally talked him into making an appearance, and as soon as he got onstage he said, "Aw, man, let me tell y'all somethin', I'm mad as a motherfucker. Niggas just came and got me out of bed at the hotel and I was in some pussy. Whole industry be tryin' to pupperize me."

THE INDUSTRY LOVED Dirty because Dirty was selling records. The whole Wu-Tang Clan was showing some crossover potential. In 1994, Wu-Tang had guest-starred on the R&B group SWV's "Anything" remix. In 1995, Ghostface guest-starred on Jodeci's "Freakin' You" and Method Man brought the R&B singer Mary J. Blige onto his remix for "I'll Be There for You/You're All I Need to Get By"—that song went platinum. Then, a few months later, Mariah Carey—one of the biggest pop stars in the world—called to ask Dirty to do a guest verse for the remix of her song "Fantasy." Mariah was a big fan of Dirty's, and she was trying to reach out to the hip-hop fan base by having Puff Daddy remix the song and Dirty do a verse on it.

Dirty said hell yeah. He went into the recording booth slurring and shouting his rhymes the same way he did every night. That's what Mariah wanted him to do, even though she said her record company was scared to death it would backfire and actually cost her some of her fans. It was a bold move for Mariah, whose image up to that point had been that of a bubblegum pop star and a classy lady. She said the execs at Columbia, her record label, asked if she'd gone crazy. They didn't want to break the formula that had worked for them, which Mariah said was to "have me sing a ballad onstage in a long dress with my hair up." But she was right. She knew adding Dirty would make that song hot.

Mariah directed the music video herself at an amusement park, which was perfect for Dirty, the way he loved going to Coney Island. You see him in the video almost as much as Mariah—Ol' Dirty Bastard dancing on the boardwalk in his flannel and boots, flashing his gold teeth. Getting on the "Fantasy" remix really helped Dirty see his appeal to the pop music fans, and the best part is he didn't change a damn thing about himself. Dirty being in that video exposed him to a whole new group of fans. Suddenly we had twelve-year-old girls in Kansas repeating Dirty's rhymes: "Me and Mariah/Go back like babies and pacifiers."

Mariah did well off it too. The "Fantasy" remix video debuted September 7, 1995, at the MTV Video Music Awards. It was the No. 1 single on the R&B charts for six weeks, and she ended her fall 1995 Madison Square Garden concert with it. Mariah left the stage and the opening bars from the remix came on. Dirty came out on the stage and did his verses.

Madison Square Garden. Dirty was that level of star now. He had money for the first time in his life. He bought his mother, Miss Cherry, a house in Park Slope, Brooklyn, and gave his father the down payment for a house in Newport News, Virginia. But more money brought more drugs. If I didn't join the party with Dirty he'd party alone. He'd run out of his coke and the nigga would wait till I went to sleep and try to grab mine off the table beside me. I'd smack his hand: "Yo, nigga, don't do that shit."

"Well, lemme get some of that liquor then."

"Sit yo' ass down. The party going to bed early tonight."

He was doing too much. He was snorting cocaine and he was smoking crack. Everyone thought me and the Brooklyn Zu were the ones encouraging Dirty's drug use, but we were the ones trying to stop him. When the nigga would turn his head we'd pour his coke on the ground and stomp it into the dirt. But he always found more. If we just took his shit, niggas would accuse us of trying to rob him. It was a catch-22—if you let him do it it's your fault he got too fucked up. If you took it from him you was known as the nigga robbin' him.

Dirty would be crying. "Just love me. This is what I do."

"Fuck that. We're not doing that."

Coke and crack became an everyday thing. When we got out of the studio at night, Dirty would give me the look. "Yo. You ready?"

And if you said no, it was goodnight to you.

I would say, "Nah, Dirty, I'll just stay here and watch you."

"I'm buying, Buddha, I'm buying. I'll get what you want."

"Look, look, man, I been awake for two days and I don't need no more of that shit." But if nobody wanted to go with him to get it, Dirty would start calling the dealers to come to his crib.

Dirty didn't take the drugs to be Ol' Dirty Bastard. Dirty took the drugs to escape a world where everybody wanted something. It was his way of having fun and enjoying himself and relaxing after so many people wanted him to come to a meeting or come to the studio or were stressing him out about shit, so every now and then he'd have some drugs and just hide and wouldn't answer the phone and wouldn't talk to nobody. He'd get high for a couple days, and then sleep, get up, order some sushi, chill, then go back to sleep. He'd wake up and order some broccoli pizza and he was good. At the end of the day, he had a lot of people wanting him to be here and be there and do this and do that and he was like, Yo, where's my private life? So you know what? If I'm not getting fucked up I just realize I gotta do this shit and I'm not having fun and I'm spending money on everyone else. And having no fun.

I used to ask him when are we gonna stop?

He said, "Motherfucker, we ain't never gonna stop. We're gonna do this shit till we're seventy."

He was getting ready to get fucked up, and I said, "All right. Okay. If that's what it's gonna be, we're gonna need to put in work, though. You can't sit there and do this shit all day, Dirty, and we don't make no money."

And I ain't gonna say it was all him by himself because some of that shit had an influence on me. I was worried about him. He was doing so much that I couldn't stand there and see him constantly do that shit, and you couldn't just take it from him, 'cause either he ain't gonna want you around no more or you the nigga stealin' his shit. So what a couple of us used to do was sit and get high with him sometimes just so he wouldn't smoke all that shit by himself and get way too fucked up. We acted like we were inhaling it all the time but he'd turn his head and we'd blow it out, pull off the weed and blow it out, because this nigga, he didn't have limits. I was trying to help Dirty get off the drugs, but any time I started to get really heavy on him about it, that's when he didn't want me around.

I started realizing how much it had been affecting me and affecting my family, and that's when I started staying away. I started staying home more. I looked at my kids and I said I can't do this anymore. So I took it out of my life.

After I stopped doing coke I became the designated Dirty-watcher. Everybody always wanted me to make sure he showed up or did this or did that. Sylvia Rhone at Elektra would call me and tell me to make sure Dirty don't mess things up with Dante Ross, or with Rick Posada or RZA. Raekwon used to call me before Wu-Tang concerts and be like, "Yo, Buddha, just make sure Dirty shows up." People I'd just met started to expect me to stay sober while Dirty got high. The night before we shot Dirty's video for the "Shimmy Shimmy Ya" remix with E-40 and MC Eiht, E-40 pulled me to the side and said, "Yo, Buddha, we gotta get Dirty in the studio at six thirty in the morning, so make sure you're standing beside him at six o'clock. Don't let that nigga out your sight. 'Cause if you let Dirty out of your sight it's a wrap."

Dirty said, "Nah, you go on home, Buddha, I'll be okay."

And I said, "*Hell* no." Any time I let Dirty out my sight he disappeared. And we was losing money.

So I was standing outside waiting to meet him at six, and I'd see him trying to creep out at five forty-five.

"Where you going?"

"Damn, come on, Buddha. I been drinking all night, I had some girls over here, I got the kids later this morning. Come on."

"Listen," I said. "You have an opportunity here. Don't blow it."

Dirty had this crazy idea he wanted to call MTV with, and I was trying to talk him out of it: "Nah, you shouldn't do that, Dirty."

"Okay, I'm gonna do it just 'cause you said I shouldn't do it."

Finally I had to sit him down and just curse him out: "Okay, look, you stupid motherfucker, you're gonna fuck this shit up. When we're sittin' here trying to figure out the next way we're gonna eat, you're gonna wish you'd listened."

"It ain't gonna happen. I'm gonna do it a way that people are gonna love it."

When Dirty got ready to do something he just did it. He didn't call me to ask permission. He would call me after he did it, but by then it was too late and the damage was done. But he'd call to ask, "How do we fix this, Buddha?"

CHAPTER 7

THAT OLD GOOD WELFARE CHEESE

Dirty put his welfare card on his album cover. That was the kind of thing Dirty did to put himself out there and let the fans know he was real. He said on Wu-Tang's "Dog Shit," "Got meals but still grill that old good welfare cheese," meaning even though he had money he was keeping it hood. He said it on his song "Raw Hide": "Who the FUCK wants to be an MC if you can't get paid to be a fuckin' MC? I came out my mama's pussy, I'm on welfare. Twenty-six years old, still on welfare." Well, after Dirty passed, his father gave an interview and said how much that line hurt and embarrassed him—he said the family was on welfare early on, but he and his wife had worked hard to get the family *off* welfare, and he couldn't understand why his son was on MTV bragging about being on it.

See, Dirty though, he was proud he was on welfare. He put his actual welfare card on the cover of his album. His dad and mom may have worked their way out of the welfare system, but once Dirty moved out on his own and married Icelene he had to go right back into it. So Dirty put his identification card for food coupons and public assistance on the cover of his album. That was his actual card, only with his name and address replaced with the name of the album. It was the greatest thing that a man could ever think of: a welfare card selling gold and platinum.

Dirty was always at the heart of what was going on. He was the product of a neighborhood where the kids grew up on welfare. I remember during President Clinton's first term he was promising to end welfare, or at least change the system to where you got two years of financial support and job training and then you were expected to find a job. "We have to end welfare as a way of life," he said in the 1994 State of the Union address, "and make it a path to independence and dignity."

But independence and dignity worked different where we was from. When you grew up on food stamps and so did most of the people you knew, there was no shame in paying for your food that way. So when Dirty came up with the idea of taking a limo to pick up his welfare check, everybody thought it was funny. We thought the *idea* was funny, but Dirty put the plan into action. He actually got on the phone and called MTV to film the whole thing. He wasn't even thinking about how it might damage him or hurt his image. Elektra had paid Dirty a $45,000 advance on his album, which was more than the income limit to stay on welfare. And there was the money from Wu-Tang Clan's album sales on top of that. But Dirty hadn't filed his taxes yet for the year so he was still collecting welfare based on his income from the previous year. He was going on TV and announcing he was a welfare cheat. I was right there, telling him, "Yo, Dirty, don't do this. I'm telling you we're gonna pay for this sometime in some way."

"Nah, you're too nervous, Buddha. Don't worry about it."

I was like, "Yo, it's my job—and I'm not even getting paid for it—to watch out for you and keep you from doing stupid shit like this."

"Why wouldn't you want to get free money? Why *not* get something from the government for a change?"

Dirty was wearing a sky blue hunting cap with earflaps, drinking liquor in the limo on the way to the check-cashing place with his wife and kids. Icelene had on sunglasses and a white hat and a puffy coat. They took little Barson, Taniqua, and little Shaquita inside and cashed their $375 welfare check and got their food stamps.

Dirty asked, "You got the camera on? It's on? Good. It's free money. Why wouldn't you want to get free money? The people that want to cut off the welfare, man, I think that's terrible. You know how hard it is for people to live without nothin'. You owe me forty acres and a mule anyway. For real. I'm in this rap game to get money. You know what I'm sayin'? I got babies. It's time to take care of my babies. I didn't think it would work. I swear. But it worked—we got food stamps!"

The second he finished saying that, I was shaking my head, like, *Dirty, oh man . . .*

Not that his message about making money was anything new for a rapper. Rappers have never been shy about making money from music. Wu-Tang said "cash rules everything around me," but before them the group name EPMD stood for Erick and Parrish Makin' Dollars. Too $hort said if they didn't pay him he'd never rap. Biggie said as a young black kid in the slums you have three ways out: "Either you're slingin' crack rock or you got a wicked jump shot," or you're rapping your way out, like Biggie and Dirty and me.

The critics complain that rap has become too much about showing off your fancy cars and expensive jewelry—and I agree that those things have distracted people from the beats and the rhymes and the stories the rappers tell—but when you look at how a lot of those rappers grew up, they never dreamed in a million years they'd have enough money to buy those cars. Why wouldn't they show them off? Dirty wasn't flashy with the money he made; he was honest about where he came from. Dirty's people were African American and Native American—America had fucked him over. Now he was just stealing back the little bit he was in the position to steal.

MTV News titled the segment "Ol' Dirty Bastard Gets Paid." It made a big splash. When it aired, me and Dirty were in Germany. We'd just finished doing one show and had arrived in the next city to get ready to do the next show. Elektra Records called and asked Dirty, "Yo, are you watching television right now?"

"No. Why?"

" 'Cause the *president* is talking about you."

Dirty said, "WHAT? Buddha, come to my room, come to my room!" We turned on MTV News and they were showing footage from a President Clinton speech, him promising welfare changes and talking about how America will not stand for people abusing the system. So it's the president of the United States talking, and then they cut to Dirty getting out of the limousine, going in to pick up his welfare check. Then they cut back to the president, talking about how we have to crack down on people getting public assistance.

And that shit just *fucked* me and Dirty up. I was sitting there like, "Yo, nigga, I *told* you not to do that. From now on you gonna start listening to what I tell you, 'cause you're gonna fuck this shit up."

Dirty's caseworker saw the MTV footage and cut off his welfare. Just picture that moment. His caseworker was maybe sitting at home having a beer and Russell Jones comes on television taking a limo to pick up his welfare check.

But in the hood, though, people loved it. When we flew back home to New York, we were walking down the street in the hood and everybody was like, "Yo, Dirty, I just got *my* food stamps. I'm on the same shit you on!"

I said, "Oh no, you see the epidemic you just started on the streets?"

Dirty said, "That's good. Now they don't gotta look at it as a bad thing. People are out here on food stamps finding a way to get that money. Steal from the rich to give to the poor. The government likely owes them this money anyway. Yo, we just helped our people. And look at it like this: for every person that says that to us that's another record sale for us. They believe in our movement."

People in the hood got what Dirty was doing, but to welfare's critics he'd just reinforced the stereotype of the welfare cheat that they were using as a platform to try to get rid of the welfare system. The politicians against welfare claimed that brothers were collecting their checks while making an unreported salary selling drugs, and that the welfare moms were having babies just so they could sit at home and collect a check instead of go out and find a job. When approached with that kind of thinking, Dirty's stunt didn't look like any kind of political statement—it only confirmed the negative stereotypes of black folks in the hood stealing money from the hardworking, taxpaying Americans. Sure, Dirty's welfare stunt sold some records, but at what cost? Dirty had always been known as wild and unpredictable for his rhyme style and his onstage persona, but the welfare check marked a turning point for him in that people who didn't even listen to rap knew his name and were waiting to see what he'd do next.

It was no coincidence that Dirty's next video would show him dressed in a straitjacket and confined to a padded room. In the public mind, Dirty became that crazy rapper who took a limo to pick up his welfare check. It became a career-defining event in a way that I think Dirty was proud of, but he wished people could see past that five-minute video to look at the rest of his message and his music. He had always put his real life into his music—he prided himself on being the same dude on his records as he was in person. But after the MTV News segment aired, he started to feel like people looked at everything he did as part of a performance. He felt like people started to look at his life as an extended publicity stunt, and there was no room left for him to be a private person.

Dream Hampton, writing in the *Village Voice,* went so far as to speculate on Dirty's sanity: "I'm not sure Ol' Dirty articulated with any clarity his politics on welfare reform. It's pretty bananas to expect clarity from hip-hop's self-proclaimed drunken bastard, I know. The question is, can insanity be revolutionary if it lives within the Black body of an unpredictable crazy motherfucker? If our nuts can't be trusted, can they be dismissed?" After Dirty took that limo ride on MTV News, the critics either wanted to call Dirty crazy or call the whole thing a publicity stunt. Either response was dismissive.

People throw that word *crazy* around too lightly when it comes to Dirty. Admittedly, he set himself up for it, calling himself crazy as he introduced himself to the world on the "Intro" track on *Return to the 36 Chambers:* "This fuckin' guy that I speak to you about is somethin' crazy. He's somethin' insane." But Method Man on "Wu-Tang: 7th Chamber" said, "I be that insane nigga from the psycho ward," and nobody calls Meth crazy. It was just another way to brag. Dirty was crazy meaning outlandish and unrestrained, not psychotic. Dirty was funny, but he was serious too. During the MTV News segment he went from drunkenly crooning the Friends of Distinction's "Check It Out" to looking directly into the camera to ask welfare's critics, "You know how hard it is for people to live without nothin'?" He might not have written a political manifesto, but the man made his point.

CHAPTER 8

GOTS LIKE COME ON THRU

Watching Dirty go through the process of becoming a bigger star made me think more about what I was doing to define myself as Buddha Monk. I benefited from my connection with Dirty, no question—I was making money onstage and in the studio with him. I was touring the world. But I didn't get into music to make records and tour *with* somebody. I got into music to make my own records and do my own tours.

Dirty had been supportive. At his shows he would even throw a Buddha Monk song onto the set list. At a show in Zurich, Switzerland, in 1995, me and Dirty did his songs "Shimmy Shimmy Ya" and "Hippa to da Hoppa," then went right into my song "Life's a Scheme." Dirty stood there onstage with me and sang my chorus the same way I'd sang his. A lot of rappers bring their boy onstage with them as hype man, but I don't know many rappers who'll stand there beside them and trade places for a minute and let them shine on their own song.

Dirty was finished recording *Return to the 36 Chambers,* so I started using some of the session time Dirty had already paid for. I used some of his time to work on producing some of the Brooklyn Zu stuff and some songs for my boys Da Manchuz. I was working on my own album, *The Prophecy*. I recorded what would become my first single, "Nightmare on Zu Street." Me and my cousin Marcus Logan had been making beats at my house on the cheap, the way Dirty used to make a beat in his bedroom. I had an MPC 2000 sampler and my partner Dean from across the street played instruments. That's how we made my song "Gots Like Come on Thru."

My connection with Dirty and Wu-Tang Clan gave me some name recognition to help me shop the single to labels. Dirty sang the hook for me, reworking a line of his from "The Stomp," which was the first song I'd helped Dirty record: "Wu, gots like come on thru. Soooh—that's the call for the Wu." Dirty did the hook for me, but I had to pay him to do it. His management ended up asking us to pay Dirty after I worked on his whole album for free. But when you're working with somebody else and they're your friend, it's not just about money or a job. I was trying to understand that the best I could: agents and managers and label execs get involved and things become more about money. Making a guest appearance on a song means asking permission from your label, then your label wants to work out payment from your friend's label. It's the way the business works—you're not your own man anymore. Wu-Tang Clan had tried to change that system by signing the group to one label and each member to a different label. They made some progress, but the industry's hard to change. Your label doesn't want you recording for another label behind their back.

I never saw that fact more clearly that when I helped bring Dirty and Busta Rhymes together on a song. They were two MCs from established groups—Dirty from Wu-Tang and Busta from Leaders of the New School—not to mention two of the wildest MCs in rap history. They were both signed to Elektra, which meant the label was 100 percent behind a collaboration, because they wouldn't have to share the money with another record company.

Initially, Dirty didn't want to do a song with Busta—he didn't have any problem with him personally, but he didn't like the fact that people were comparing him to Busta when he wanted to have an original sound to his rap. Some people said Dirty borrowed his gruff voice from Busta, and Dirty thought it seemed corny to him to respond to that criticism by teaming up with the rapper he was being compared to. But I knew if he and Busta did it right it would come out hot, and putting them back to back on a song would show people they really did have a different sound and style—they both had gruff voices, but Busta didn't mix singing and rapping the way Dirty did, and Dirty didn't do Busta's speed raps. Their deliveries were totally different.

Dirty and Busta were both Elektra recording artists, but the label couldn't get them together. It took me and my man Joaquim to get them together. Joaquim was cool with Busta and he knew I was cool with Dirty, so he called me one day to say, "Yo, Busta Rhymes is about to record a remix of his song 'Woo Hah!!' and he's looking for someone to do a guest verse. I need to ask you a question, Buddha—how do you think a song with Busta and Dirty would do?"

"Dirty and Busta? I think if they did a song together that shit would go out the box."

That's when another voice came on the line and said, "Buddha Monk, I appreciate that shit. That's exactly what I'm tryin' to tell everybody right now."

"Who the fuck is this?" I asked.

Joaquim said, "Yo, that's Busta on the phone."

"Busta Rhymes?" I asked. "Yo, man, what's up?" Busta was already a big rap star from his two albums with Leaders of the New School and his legendary guest verse on A Tribe Called Quest's "Scenario."

"I need you to do me a favor," said Busta. "I need you to get with Dirty and make this song happen."

"Word, I can talk to Dirty for you."

"Yo, Buddha, if you do that for me, I promise you I'll be in debt. When you get your album I'll do a song with you, whatever you need."

"All right, bet. Good lookin' out." I was a rapper without a record deal, trying to get his first solo album signed. He was Busta Rhymes, international rap star. A guest appearance from Busta Rhymes would be exactly what I needed to attract a label's attention.

So I talked to Dirty. When I brought the track to Dirty he was staying at the Renaissance Hotel in Manhattan. They'd just started putting CD players in the hotel rooms. "Let me play you this track, Dirty. Busta wants you to get on it. It's a perfect opportunity because people be going around saying you sound like Busta or he sounds like you. This way you can both get on the same track and show everybody that y'all are both on a whole different page. Put the two of you side by side and let people hear there's no father to either one of your styles." Dirty started listening to the beat. He got into it, started nodding his head. He got in touch with Busta and they scheduled some studio time.

When the studio date came around, a blizzard had hit New York. Busta Rhymes came to pick me up at my house in Brooklyn. I looked out the window and saw his burgundy Range Rover turn down my block, which they hadn't plowed that morning. Busta drove about halfway down my block before he got stuck in the snow so deep that it fucked up his transmission.

Now, Busta's got on diamond watches, standing in the middle of the street trying to figure out what we're gonna do to get us to the studio. I came outside. All my friends came outside. The whole block came outside. We had fifteen people trying to help dig Busta Rhymes's car out of the snow. The car couldn't reverse but it could still go forward a bit, so we had people shoveling from the middle of the block all the way back to the street so we could get him to the next corner, Rochester and Sterling.

He went to park the car in a lot and call a tow truck to pick it up, and then we had to catch a cab. By this time Dirty had done left the studio. He was at the hotel with a girl. So I said, damn, now I gotta get Dirty back in the studio and go through this whole process again.

BUSTA CALLED ME the next day, "Yo, Buddha, I lost my pager."

"What you mean you lost your pager?"

"I lost my pager on your block when we was shoveling snow."

Then one of the girls from my block, Tootie, found the pager and brought it to me, saying, "I think this is Busta's pager because mad pages keep comin' up saying Busta Rhymes."

I called Busta. "I got your pager."

"You gotta be kidding me."

"No, one of my people on the block picked it up."

"Yo, Buddha. That's love. That kind of thing doesn't happen. People usually would just keep it or try to sell it."

"Nah, my people on the block's not like that. They respect your music."

Then we finally got to the studio, got Dirty to come back to the studio, and Busta and Dirty recorded their verses.

TWO WEEKS LATER we flew out to California to shoot the video. As soon as we landed I went clothes shopping because I was excited to be in the video. We arrived in California the night before the shoot, and the next morning Busta called me to get Dirty up and get him to the set. Dirty was drunk as hell. He'd been up all night drinking, and he was tired. He wasn't trying to do no video. The director was steady pumping Dirty with coffee and Dirty was like, "No, I don't want no more of that shit. I need *liquor* to stay up."

The set was designed like a mental ward. The video opens with a nurse pushing a cart full of meds—he opens a door labeled "High Risk" and there's Dirty and Busta in straitjackets, chained together at the feet in a padded room. "The straitjackets were Busta's idea," Busta's main man Spliff Star told me. "Busta always stitched and sewed his own clothing for his videos. Busta's crazy. He watches a *lot* of cartoons. Up to this day he's addicted to cartoons, so maybe that's where he gets his ideas. The two girls that's in the 'Woo Hah!!' remix video, Dirty found them at a 7-Eleven. He picked them off the street, like, 'Come here, girl. You know who I am? You gonna be in my video.' And they went to the shoot with us and danced in the video."

I thought I was going to be in the video, but the way that Busta did it had no need for Dirty's boys or any of Busta's Flipmode Squad to be in the video. So I'm sittin' on the sidelines with Spliff Star and Busta's cousin Rampage the Last Boy Scout. They flew me out there and I didn't even get in the video.

Worse, back in New York when I came to see Busta to get him to do a verse on my album, he didn't even want to let me upstairs. Joaquim was working in the studio with Busta when I called to get buzzed up, and Busta was like, "Tell him I'm not here. Tell him I went home already." Joaquim reminded him, though. He said, "You wouldn't have had that song with Dirty if it weren't for Buddha."

So in the end Busta said, "Right—let Buddha upstairs."

He even came back to my house to hear some of the beats I was working on. "Damn, these are your beats?" He was listening to my beats and freestyling over them. He picked the song he liked best and said, "This is the one. When you're ready to do that song together, let me know."

But when I got back to him he said, "Yo, dawg, Elektra won't let me do it." Again, that's the industry. *The record label won't let me do it* is the excuse you always hear. But I didn't really believe that. Busta had been doing a lot of songs with a lot of people, but all the sudden Sylvia Rhone was putting a real tight noose around him?

"Won't *let* you?"

"Yeah, Sylvia won't let me."

But I kept hearing mad new songs come out with Busta Rhymes on them.

If I had been signed to Elektra, that excuse wouldn't have made any sense anymore, because Sylvia wouldn't have a damn thing against Busta—one of Elektra's biggest stars—doing a guest verse to help another Elektra artist sell records. This is where Dirty stepped in and tried to help me out. He had a meeting with Sylvia Rhone to follow up on the song he'd recorded with Busta. He came back to the studio with a smile on his face. "Guess what, Buddha?"

"What?"

"Sylvia says they're thinking about offering a record deal to this dude Buddha Monk."

"Get the fuck out of here."

By then I had finished two of my solo tracks and taken them to Elektra, so Sylvia had heard my track "Gots Like Come on Thru" that I made with my cousin Marcus.

Dirty even asked RZA to go with him to meet with Sylvia to put in a word for me and get my record deal pinned down. They were supposed to vouch for me as an artist and commit to working with me on it. Dirty was going to guest on some tracks and RZA contribute to the production. I could have got a real solid deal with their names attached.

But they never showed up. Elektra ended up giving the deal to Busta's cousin Rampage the Last Boy Scout, in part because Busta was 100 percent committed to backing his cousin. Busta appeared on three tracks on that album. I ain't mad at Rampage because he'd paid his dues backing Busta for years, rhyming on albums by Busta and his Flipmode Squad. That was how it was supposed to work—you pay your dues as part of somebody's team and when the time is right they help lift you up and get you your deal and give you your shine. I wasn't mad at Rampage, but as far as RZA and Dirty went, I was in a rage.

I was in a rage but there was only so much I could show Dirty. We were old friends, but he was treating me like a business associate, and I still had to live off the money I made doing studio work and tours with him. I had kids to support. It wasn't like I could tell him to fuck off and burn that bridge. Plus, in Dirty's mind he'd just missed another meeting. If you think he was bad for not showing up to the concerts, you should see his track record with meetings! But Dirty missing that meeting was enough to convince Elektra that Dirty wasn't 100 percent devoted to my album, and that was enough to make them move on to the next rapper.

All the work was beginning to catch up with me. I'd go home and spend time with my family for one day, then go back to the studio for four or five days. Go home and spend one day with the family before we headed out on tour again.

I needed to be more of a family man for Patricia and my kids. I understand that. But at the same time when you're not making money like the main guy is, you gotta be flexible enough to be there at the studio at all times—that's how you're gonna be able to feed your family. I didn't want my kids to grow up without me, but I felt like I had to choose between paying the bills or being a broke family man sitting in the house with his girl mad 'cause he's *not* paying the bills. I thought making the money and being responsible would be enough. It wasn't.

I was busting my ass every day working hard, but Patricia knew the stories of Ol' Dirty Bastard on tour and assumed that I was out fucking groupies too. Then I came back home from tour and started noticing the pussy felt different. I had to ask her, "Are you fucking somebody?"

Come to find out she was seeing the nigga that she went with before me. With me on the road, she had gone back to the nigga. I caught them at her sister's house. I kicked the door in and everything. I bent the shit outta that door. The nigga was in there. I grabbed a knife from the kitchen and said, "How you wanna go? You wanna go out the window or you wanna get stabbed in your ass? I'll give you the choice."

But I didn't do it, because it takes two, you know, and I hadn't been home the way she wanted me home. I didn't do shit to her, either. I stayed with her for a while longer, trying to maybe change things and put us back on the right track. That didn't work. We split up and went our own ways.

These were the problems that came with making a living at music, but as the stakes got higher I had to ask myself if this was the living I'd set out to make. It was one of my lowest moments. I felt fucked over by Patricia, fucked over by Busta, fucked over by Elektra, and RZA, and worst of all, Dirty.

ME AND DIRTY ON TOUR
IN GERMANY, 1995.

OL' DIRTY BASTARD, RICK POSADA,
SPIRITUAL ASSASSIN FROM DA MANCHUZ (*IN
THE BACKGROUND*), ME, AND JACK HERSCA
AT CHUNG KING STUDIOS IN MANHATTAN
WORKING ON *RETURN TO THE 36 CHAMBERS:
THE DIRTY VERSION* (1995).

BROOKLYN ZU OUT TO SUPPORT DIRTY FOR
A SHOW AT NEW YORK'S PALLADIUM, 1995.
FRONT ROW: CHANNEL LIVE (HAKEEN GREEN
AND VINCENT "TUFFY" MORGAN), MILKBONE;
MIDDLE ROW: ME, DIRTY; *BACK ROW:* TWELVE
O'CLOCK, RAISON THE ZUKEEPER.

Brooklyn Zu logo.

OL' DIRTY BASTARD WITH MIKE D AND MCA
FROM THE BEASTIE BOYS BACKSTAGE AT A WU-
TANG CLAN/RAGE AGAINST THE MACHINE SHOW
IN THE CONTINENTAL AIRLINES ARENA, EAST
RUTHERFORD, NEW JERSEY, AUGUST 20, 1997.
PHOTO © BY RICKY POWELL #THELAZYHUSTLER

ALL GROWN UP: BARSON JONES,
AKA YOUNG DIRTY BASTARD,
AND SHAQUITA JONES, 2011.

K-BLUNT AND 5-FOOT HYPER
SNIPER OF THE ZU NINJAZ IN
WILLINGBORO, NEW JERSEY,
2003.

An advertisement for Haldol, the drug prescribed to Dirty in prison. *Archives of General Psychiatry*, 1974.

Dirty and me onstage at Plaid, Manhattan, 2003, at a welcome-home party sponsored by Vice.

REUNITING WITH THE REMAINING MEMBERS OF WU-TANG CLAN FOR A PERFORMANCE AT THE 2004 MONTREUX JAZZ FESTIVAL IN SWITZERLAND, WHERE I WAS LIVING IN THE WAKE OF DIRTY'S DEATH.

Ghostface Killah, GZA, and me.

Raekwon and me.

RZA and me.

METHOD MAN AND ME.

INSPECTAH DECK AND ME.

ME IN FRONT OF THE ALPS,
VERBIER, SWITZERLAND, 2008.

DIRTY'S UNCLE PETE,
WITH GZA IN THE
BACKGROUND, PERFORMING
"WU-REVOLUTION" IN
PHILADELPHIA WITH THE
REMAINING MEMBERS OF
WU-TANG, 2008.

AFTER DIRTY'S PASSING, MEMORIALS POPPED UP AROUND THE WORLD.

Toronto, 2009.

A painting from Rumpage Skate Park, Bridgeport, Connecticut, 2013.

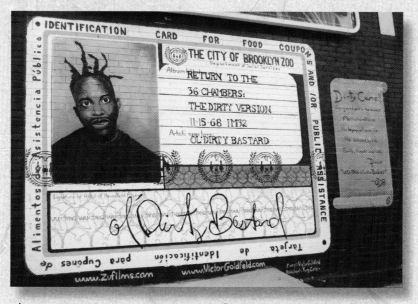

A mural at the corner of Putnam and Franklin Avenues in Bedford-Stuyvesant, Brooklyn, near where me and Dirty lived as teenagers.

Onstage in Germany, 2006.

Atlantis and me, 2013.

CHAPTER 9

ESCAPE TO WILLINGBORO

Dirty was going through his own relationship troubles. He fought with Icelene over money and groupies. And when Dirty fought with Icelene, he'd go stay with one of his other girls. It got to the point that he and Icelene spent more time together unhappy than happy. Icelene had turned a blind eye to the other girls for as long as she could, but now the kids were getting old enough to understand what their daddy was doing. Icelene told a reporter that Barson had caught his father in bed with another woman. Money was another issue—Icelene claimed she had to argue with Dirty to get him to give money to her and the kids while he was out spending thousands on liquor, cocaine, and groupies. "He gives me what he wants when he wants," she told the reporter. "He's living good and we're not." She knew about the luxury apartment he kept with Belinda in Jersey City. She knew about the Beverly Hills mansion where he'd stay with the Wu-Tang Clan while she and the kids still lived in an apartment in Bed-Stuy. The newspapers began calling him a deadbeat dad.

Dirty and Icelene separated in 1995. I know it hurt Dirty. It had to. They'd been together since they were teenagers. Icelene moved herself and the kids out to Long Island, enrolled the kids in a good school system, and signed Barson up for Little League. She was trying to grow and become the woman she needed to be, while Dirty was trying to be the same Russell Jones he'd been growing up in Brooklyn and at the same time be Ol' Dirty Bastard the rap star. Dirty wasn't in the right state of mind for Long Island. He just didn't fit in there—just coming to visit the kids, he showed up drunk and rowdy to the Little League games.

They never officially got divorced—Dirty was convinced it was just a matter of time before things would work out. He said it was like Moses parting the Red Sea: at some point it had to come back together. Icelene felt that way too. "I just want him to get some help," she said. "Find your way home, because I'm still here. Hopefully he'll wake up before it's too late." She was so close to him that she saw the problems before the rest of us did, but the separation took a toll on him. After Dirty and Icelene separated he became even less interested in coming in to work in the studio. Dirty had always said he got into the rap game to make money, but he started to back out of shows even when he knew he was losing money. When we were already on tour, thousands of miles away from home, I used to have to talk him into going onstage because he'd just want to stay in the hotel. I said, "Dirty, you know I'm only making five hundred dollars a show, right?" and sometimes that would get him out there to perform. But sometimes he'd just give me the money and we'd stay at the hotel.

We'd arrive in a city to play a show, Dirty would meet a girl, and if the chick was bad we'd wind up staying for two or three days, knowing we had a show the next fucking day in a different town. This nigga just didn't give a fuck. "I already made fifty thousand, what the fuck I need to go and do the last two shows for with fifty thousand in my pocket?"

"But you can have seventy thousand in your pocket if you go."

"Nah, I don't feel like going."

"But didn't we get paid an advance for these shows?"

"Yeah, we'll just send it back. Don't worry about it."

I'd talk to him real quiet and serious. "Dirty, we need to keep traveling. Because I ain't making money like you're making. I can't take off the way you can. You understand? Every show that you do is money for me. If you do six shows, I go home with three thousand dollars in my pocket, as opposed to you going home with sixty thousand in your pocket. I really need these shows." And that convinced him to get back on the road, until he figured out he could just stay at the hotel and pay me out of his own pocket for the shows that we didn't do.

Getting paid to stay at the hotel sounded fine to me. My relationship back home was over, so I was running through girls like a train conductor. Next stop: hallway. Round trip: elevator.

But I wasn't in a good place. Dirty and I were both hurting. He was drinking heavily, and I was back to matching him drink for drink. Why should I be the sober one trying to keep us on track?

I was tired of being the designated Dirty-watcher. And Dirty was just plain tired. We loved making music but we'd lost sight of our goal. We needed a break.

So we escaped. We knew just where to go. The best times that Dirty had was not in New York or Brooklyn. They was in Willingboro, New Jersey, where K-Blunt and the Zu Ninjaz lived. Willingboro became our headquarters, because in New York Dirty had a lot of people always coming to him about money, people always getting on his nerves. So he decided to get out of New York. We hopped into Dirty's Benz with the supersystem that could rattle windows a block away. On our way out of the city Dirty swung by my brother Born's work, ran inside, and came back out with Born. Born said, "This nigga just kidnapped me from work. Threw some money at them and told them I wouldn't be back for two or three days." Shit, he kept Born out in Jersey for two or three *weeks*.

In Willingboro we felt like we were with family. We could spend two Gs in one night for liquor and cocaine or whatever, and people out there would say, "No, you're spending too much money."

Dirty said, "No, you think I'm worried about this? I'm gonna do two shows tomorrow and get it back."

When Dirty had messed things up with his family at home, everybody in Jersey became his new family. "It's official now. Niggas is branded," Dirty used to say. "Niggas is branded." Like a herd of cattle. That's what that Wu-Tang *W* is, it's a brand. Covers the whole affiliates, top to bottom. Our Jersey connection was the Zu Ninjaz: Irie, Popa Chief, and K-Blunt. Those are my boys. We were staying at the Gate, which is what we called the house where Irie lived with his girl, Lisa Miller. It was Lisa's house and at first she was cool with letting us stay there and do our thing. Lisa was our scientist. Anything with a computer she'd get done in twenty seconds. She can take a computer apart and put it back together and it'll work just fine.

Dirty used to love driving in the back of that house, through the field, with his Benz. He didn't want to park it in front of the house 'cause he didn't want nobody to know he was there. But we came to see that out in Jersey people didn't treat Dirty like some kind of superstar. We brought people from the street into our circle, and they looked out for us, protected us not because we were rappers but because we could be real with them.

Dirty felt like he could talk about his problems with them. One night he said, "Man, I don't know if I can do this shit no more."

"What do you mean? This rap shit?" I asked him.

Dirty was more depressed than I'd ever seen him. Blunt told him, "Listen, we don't want to hear that bullshit. You ain't going to quit rappin'. You just need to take some time off to remember what you love about music and why you got into this career to begin with."

"Yo, Blunt, I just feel like the fish in the fishbowl, like I'm by myself in this fishbowl and people coming round staring at me like I'm a goddamn alien or some shit."

It's hard to be a character all the time. People would see Dirty on the street and they'd expect him to be the same Ol' Dirty Bastard he was onstage or on TV.

While Dirty was taking some time off in Willingboro, everybody back in New York was calling me to ask where he was. Everybody knew to call Buddha. I was the middleman. But this time around, instead of me trying to convince Dirty to call people back or show up where they wanted him to, I just played dumb. Everybody called me in Willingboro to ask where Dirty was and I'd tell them, "I don't know."

"Don't lie. Don't fuckin' lie. I know you know where he is."

Elektra would call looking for him. RZA would call. Icelene would call, and I heard Dirty finally call her back and yell at her over the phone: "Don't be calling me for no fuckin' money." Once you split up they start calling you because they don't have as much access to it like they did when they was with you.

Dirty hated going home to New York because there was so much love in Jersey. We'd hang out as late as we could, until six or seven in the morning when some of our friends had to head into work. Dirty would stretch and yawn and ask me, "What are we doing today?"

"Getting fucked up," I'd tell him. "Same as yesterday. We're gonna sit here and order some food and get drunk. Maybe play some cards." At night we'd go to the club. And when we went we went deep. I'm talking about cars following cars following cars. Twenty or thirty people walking into the club. This was beyond family—Dirty and I were separated from our families but in Jersey we found nothing but love.

Plus, it was good for our music. Dirty and I were sick and tired of the music industry, but weren't trying to quit making music. At the Gate we had a secret room upstairs where we'd shut the door, turn up the music, smoke weed, and write mad rhymes. We wrote notebooks full of rhymes. And we'd try them out on each other before we'd go to the studio. Then we'd get after each other there, too. "No, that's not the rhyme. That's not how you did it at the house."

K-Blunt knew how to come in with some energy. You can hear it on his first verse on the Zu Ninjaz song "Slicer." He'd stomp into the booth like, "Fuck that. This is how you do it. Yo, turn my shit up, Buddha."

But even with Blunt sometimes, he'd go in there ready to show the world and I'd still be like, "*Delete.* Do it again. Turn the page, nigga. Delete." He'd do it to me too. That's how we learned to rhyme better and take it to the next level. We battled each other all the time. That's the way we would improve our craft.

MY RELATIONSHIP WITH Patricia was over, so out in Jersey I had Ruth, Angie, Denise, plus Drea, a light-skinned girl with a big ass. But there was only one Mikki. I had such a crush on her. I was in love with Mikki when

Mikki was in love with everybody else. She had so many men chasing her she had to play defense. "Bob and weave," she'd tell me. "Some nigga tried to pin me up in the park, but I had to keep it moving."

Mikki's a singer. She's a little thing. Funniest shit, though, the smallest ladies are the most dangerous. She kicked Lisa's ass one time, when Lisa started getting jealous because Mikki was hanging with Dirty and us all the time. "Listen, I'm not supposed to tell you like this, but I done been in the military and everything, so y'all bitches better fall back before I fuck you up." Lisa and her are about the same size, but Lisa was a little more diesel. So Lisa kept talking, blah blah blah.

Mikki said, "I ain't even here for you. I'm here for Dirty and Buddha."

Lisa said, "Well you don't have to worry about that, 'cause I got them."

Blunt and me was on our way back from New York, and we got a phone call that Lisa went in Mikki's room and took some shit out. We was like, "Fuck that bitch up. Kick that bitch ass."

I told Mikki straight up, I said, "If you don't kick her ass I'm cuttin' you off."

Mikki said, "You know I'm gonna really hurt her if I do this. She's not gonna win. She's gonna get hurt."

"Yeah, whatever, just do what you can."

Lisa was in the kitchen cooking. Mikki went to try to talk to her woman to woman.

Blunt came in and said, "Fuck that. Y'all talking too much. Fuck all that talking shit. Let's get to it."

"Why'd you go in my room?"

"This is my house, bitch. I go in any room I please."

She hit Mikki first, knocked her glasses off, and that was the only hit she got in. Mikki wasn't lying to me. She fucked that girl up. She had her on the ground. We had to pull her off. "Get her off of me. Get this bitch!"

After Lisa got her ass whooped, Dirty said, "Yo, y'all were wrong for that, G. You shouldn't have told Mikki to go up there and beat that girl's ass like that. She lets us stay here at her house and everything."

Wasn't long after that Lisa started talking about us fucking up her house and not helping pay the electric bills. Mikki told me and Dirty, "You got to move. You got to get up out of here."

She was right, but Dirty and I didn't listen. We kept running up the electric bills and the Brooklyn Zu kept crashing Dirty's cars. They were some bang-'em-up niggas. K-Blunt and 12 O'Clock fucked up Dirty's Benz and tried to get it fixed before he found out. Blunt tore off the whole front end of that car.

It was Blunt, Merdoc, and 12. They'd stolen the car from Dirty while he was asleep, and the first thing Dirty did when he woke up was call Blunt and say, "I know you took my car, motherfucker. I'm a kill all you motherfuckers." Blunt hung up but Dirty kept calling him back. "I'm telling you, K-Blunt, if you don't bring me my car . . ."

"I don't got your car, man. As for 12 and Merdoc I ain't even with them." But really he rode with them all the way to Philly. 12 ran into a pole and tore off the front end of that Benz. Cracked the whole windshield and everything. 12 was outside the car crying. "He's gonna kill us, G. Dirty's gonna kill all of us."

"No, he's gonna kill *you*," Blunt said. "I didn't have shit to do with it. I ain't even here. I already told him I ain't with y'all."

Blunt called his man who ran a shop at Fifty-fourth and Market in Philly, and the dude came with his tow truck and got the car. He opened up his shop at midnight and had the car fixed by 8 A.M.: repaired, painted, and everything.

When they got back to Willingboro that morning Dirty was waiting on the porch. He took one look at the car and said, "What happened to the car?"

"What you mean?"

"Well, the paint's still wet, G. What happened to the car?"

AS CRAZY A time as we were having in Willingboro, I still say it put me and Dirty back on track with our music. Not only writing new rhymes and battling each other to see whose were best, but just spending some time away from New York and the music industry. It reminded us what was fun about music. It reminded me what I'd been missing by turning it too much into a job. Working with Dirty paid my bills, but taking on the responsibility for making sure he did his work had taken a toll on our friendship. It was good just to hang out as friends again and chill with our boys and have fun. We were rejuvenated and ready to enter a new phase of our music careers.

Then it happened. September 7, 1996—Tupac Shakur, one of the biggest rappers in the world, was shot in a drive-by shooting in Las Vegas. Pac was leaving a Mike Tyson fight in the passenger seat of a BMW driven by Death Row Records owner Suge Knight. As they sat in traffic, a Cadillac pulled up beside them on the passenger side and opened fire on Tupac. Bullets hit him in his hand, his thigh, and his chest. When Dirty and I heard the news we couldn't believe it. Not because Pac had been shot—he'd been shot before. But that a car was able to pull up beside him in Vegas fight-night traffic, shoot him, and get away without being identified. There were hundreds of people right there at the scene, and here we are, almost twenty years later, and his murder is still unsolved. Conspiracy theories about Pac's death persist to this day, and the conspiracy theorists will remind you that after he'd been shot the first time in New York, Pac was known to always wear a bulletproof vest. But he didn't wear it that night.

We didn't expect Tupac to die. It took a lot out of us to hear he'd been shot, but we expected the nigga to make it. The next few days we kept MTV on in the house. They interrupted playing Tupac's videos only long enough to provide updates on his condition. On September 8 he had one surgery, and another on September 9. He survived the surgeries but remained in a drug-induced coma. Then, on September 13, 1996, Tupac died from his gunshot wounds. He was twenty-five years old.

A lot of people looked at Pac's life and said well, you live by the sword, you die by the sword. Pac rhymed about a lot of positive things, but his music was also focused on violence and death and revenge. You could already see Tupac's murder changing Dirty's way of thinking. When Pac was gunned down, it made Dirty stop and think about the message he was putting out to the world.

CHAPTER 10

RESTORATION

On September 22, 1996, nine days after Tupac's death, Dirty attended the Day of Atonement at the Nation of Islam's Mosque No. 7—the mosque Malcolm X once led—up in Harlem, where rappers and fans gathered to talk about how to make sense of Pac's death and what lessons to learn from it. The Nation of Islam's Minister Conrad Muhammad promoted the meeting by telling the *New York Times*, "There's nothing we can do to bring Tupac back, but there are tens of thousands who admire him. This meeting is to give some clarity to his life so they won't immortalize the worst of him and try to imitate that." It was a day for hip-hop to promote peace and atone for its sins.

Dirty was joined at the meeting by rappers like Fat Joe, Q-Tip, Doug E. Fresh, Lord Jamar from Brand Nubian, Spinderella from Salt-n-Pepa, and hip-hop's trio of founding fathers: Afrika Bambaataa, Grandmaster Flash, and Kool Herc. Hip-hop's elder statesmen had been complaining to the press about the more violent, more materialistic, and more misogynist turn hip-hop had taken since their generation. Fans complained that hip-hop had gone from a positive movement of the people to a negative vehicle that promoted nothing but negativity, guns, and drugs. Some people even saw Pac's murder as a case of the chickens coming home to roost.

But the event was designed to honor Tupac, not villainize him. Minister Muhammed said, "We're not honoring a gangsta rapper today—we're honoring a black man that has been murdered." He said record companies were at fault for "depicting us as uncontrollable savages so that when they kill us they won't have anybody to say that it's wrong," but he reminded the rappers in the crowd of their own role in perpetuating such negative stereotypes. We can't blame the record executives for Tupac's death without implicating ourselves, Minister Muhammed reminded the crowd. "His blood is on your hands," he said. "We must save the lives of other Tupac Shakurs out there in the world."

Other musicians took the opportunity to say a few words about Pac. The teenage singer Aaliyah said Pac was "an insightful hip-hop figure, a young artist that wrote songs that stood not only as good music but as social commentary." Dirty stood up in front of the crowd of six hundred people to say a few words and announce that he'd changed his name to Osirus. "Ol' Dirty Bastard is dead. Osirus lives!" He said he did it for the kids: "I go to the schools in my area to talk, and when the kids call me Ol' Dirty, it makes me feel bad. I always tell them about righteous things, but the mothers be looking at me funny 'cause of my name." Dirty's changing his name to Osirus had some symbolism behind it. In Egyptian mythology, Osiris was the ruler of the underworld, the god of the dead. But he wasn't just associated with death—he was the god who brought things back to life, the god of rebirth who made the Nile flow and the vegetation grow. Changing his name to Osirus was Dirty's way of saying he was changing his approach to rap music. He wanted to be reborn.

Being shot on the street in Brooklyn had made Dirty feel like a target, and Tupac's murder heightened his sense that somebody was after him. Dirty always felt that the government had something to do with Tupac's death because of the messages he was putting out. Pac's lyrics had been critical of the police, anti-hip-hop activist C. Delores Tucker, and Vice

President Dan Quayle. Dirty was convinced Pac's politics had made him a marked man. He told me, "The government always wants to shut up somebody who can reach the masses. They'll make it look like two people are rivals and present it on television that way, like they're out there making enemies so there's no telling who might have done them in. But in the background the government has their hands all tied up in it." Dirty even saw a conspiracy in the fact that Puff Daddy and the Notorious B.I.G.— who Tupac had blamed the first time he'd been shot—were scheduled to appear at the Day of Atonement but canceled at the last minute.

Then, six months after Tupac's murder, on March 9, 1997—my twenty-eighth birthday—the Notorious B.I.G. was killed out in L.A. I didn't even feel like celebrating my birthday. And if Dirty was paranoid before, he was *mad* paranoid after Pac and Biggie died. Dirty said on MTV, "Everybody scared of the government because they killed Tupac and they killed Biggie Smalls. I've been afraid of the government for twenty-nine years, but all that's dead to me now." It was a dark statement—he was tired of being afraid of what might happen to him, and ready to accept his fate. After Tupac survived that first shooting, his music had showed a new focus on his own mortality and the inevitability of his early death. Getting shot had made Dirty afraid of walking down the street in Brooklyn, made him feel vulnerable to attack when he toured and played shows, so like Pac he became more fixated on leaving behind a legacy.

That kind of talk started spooking me, because the more I started to look at the situation the more Dirty seemed to make sense. And he wasn't the only rapper looking at what happened to Tupac and Biggie and wondering who'd be next.

IN 1997, THINGS were changing for hip-hop. Two of our biggest stars had been murdered within six months of each other. Things were changing within the Wu-Tang Clan too. Wu-Tang's second group album, *Wu-Tang Forever,* was about to drop. So many of the members had become solo stars, it was tough for RZA to bring them back together as a team. The press was speculating it might not even happen. When *Vibe* magazine asked Dirty about it, he told the reporter, "I can never be out of Wu-Tang.

We blood. I would've never been anything if it wasn't for Wu-Tang, I just be going off on my own shit. Dirty just be missing in action, but it's all good. I just don't like doing the publicity stuff too much. All that extra shit is difficult for me. I'm the wrong motherfucker to be asking questions, because I don't give a fuck about all that shit." Wu-Tang Clan had not released a group album in four years, since their debut, *Enter the Wu-Tang (36 Chambers)*. In that time, Wu-Tang members Method Man, GZA, Rae-kwon, Ghostface Killah, and Ol' Dirty Bastard had released solo albums. It was an unprecedented move for a group to splinter with the intention of coming back together stronger than ever, and fans weren't sure it could happen.

Wu-Tang Clan released their new single, "Triumph," and killed all that negativity. Dirty opened "Triumph" by directly addressing the speculation that he was no longer invested in the group: "What? Y'all thought y'all wasn't gon' see me? I'm the Osirus of this shit. Wu-Tang is here forever, motherfuckers!" Osirus became one name among many. Fans still called him Ol' Dirty Bastard and his mama still called him Rusty, but he proclaimed himself Osirus to let people know he and Wu-Tang Clan were back for a whole new era, and they were doing it their own way, sending the radio stations a six-minute-long single made up of nine verses and no chorus.

Wu-Tang Clan's double album *Wu-Tang Forever* came out in June 1997, only three months after Biggie was killed, and debuted at No. 1 on the *Billboard* 200. RZA put Popa Wu and his and Dirty's uncle Pete on the intro track, "Wu Revolution." They present Wu-Tang as the forerunners of a Five Percent revolution, a group here to teach the children the truth. "Why do we kill each other?" asks Uncle Pete. "Look at our children. What kind of a future?"

Popa Wu says Wu-Tang is here give their listeners the training to see past this self-hatred. Wu-Tang is the Five Percent here to teach the 85 percent, the uncivilized, the deaf, dumb, and blind. "I'm calling my black woman a bitch," says Popa Wu. "I'm calling my peoples all kinds of things that they not. I'm lost, brother. Can you help me?" These were strong messages to open an album that goes on to have Dirty scream on the second track, "I be fucking bitches by the chunk." Dirty was supposed to be part of the group doing the teaching, but he sounded as lost and misguided as anyone.

This was the trick of bringing back together a nine-member group. Not everyone was on the same page. With a double album, there was plenty of room for all nine Wu-Tang members to shine. RZA produced all but seven of the album's twenty-nine tracks. Inspectah Deck produced "Visionz," 4th Disciple produced four songs, and True Master produced two. All of the nine Wu-Tang members—plus the unofficial tenth member, Cappadonna—rapped. Dirty did mostly intros and choruses, except for his verse on "Reunited" and the song that truly showcased his rhyming, "Dog Shit," which Dirty was the only member who rapped on. It was like he was part of Wu-Tang but even on the Wu-Tang album he was doing his own thing.

You have to understand, RZA was doing something no one had done before. To bring back together a nine-member group after five of them had made it big as solo stars was unheard of. I mean, Method Man had already won a Grammy as a solo artist. But RZA got them back into the studio, back onto the set for the video shoot (well, except Dirty, who ditched filming the "Triumph" video), and got the Wu-Tang Clan back on tour. A lot of the Wu-Tang members were pissed off because RZA had signed them up for a stadium tour as coheadliners with Rage Against the Machine, instead of teaming up with another hip-hop group or just going out on a Wu-Tang tour. Dirty didn't care. Dirty just wanted to tour. Money was money. Dirty got along with everybody, so he didn't care who he went on tour with. As long as he was getting money to feed his family, he just wanted the chance to show the world that he was a great artist.

RZA's plan was to tour with Rage to expand Wu-Tang's fan base even further. You had one of the biggest rock groups at the time headlining along with the biggest rap group. This was an arena tour. The tour made the cover of *Rolling Stone*. Rage saw it as some kind of mission of solidarity, because at that time promoters were becoming less sure about backing hip-hop tours. Too much to worry about with security, and the big insurance companies would not even write policies for a hip-hop arena show. And Wu-Tang had a bad reputation in particular. Some of it was deserved. Wu-Tang Clan members did miss a lot of shows—it was rare to see all nine of them onstage in one night, and Dirty was the worst for ditching shows. And Wu-Tang did like to see niggas in the crowd go wild and start whoopin' ass.

Their stage set for this tour with Rage Against the Machine . . . oh my God, they was rapping in front of a cop car crashed through a liquor store window. A journalist described it as a portable ghetto. After the show in Chicago a bunch of Wu members *allegedly* beat the shit out of some dude from the record label because he'd said some shit they didn't like in a radio interview. They got investigated for inciting a riot at the Deer Creek Amphitheater in Indianapolis. Allegedly they were one song into their set and somebody got on the mic and told the crowd to come on down—this enormous amphitheater and Wu-Tang invited the whole crowd onstage. Probably five thousand people rushed toward the stage. Turns out in Indiana they call that inciting a riot. So the crowd's trampling each other to jump onstage, then at the same time backstage you had cops rushing in ready to arrest Wu-Tang. But Rage managed to sneak them out the back.

With Wu-Tang you didn't just have to worry about the crowd rioting during the show—you had to worry about how pissed off they'd get when Dirty or Method Man *didn't* show up. That's how the tour fell apart. When Wu-Tang began in 1992 it was nine hungry dudes all on equal footing trying to make it in the music business, but by 1997 you had a stage full of niggas who were each one a superstar. Each one thinking, Shit, if Dirty don't have to show up why the fuck should I have to show up either? Nine egos were too big to keep under control. Dirty stopped showing up. But this time he wasn't the only one. At one show there was no Dirty, the next there was no Dirty or Method Man. Then the next there was no Method Man, no GZA, and of course, no Dirty. A few weeks into it the entire Wu-Tang Clan missed two shows in a row, and then that was it. Wu-Tang left the tour.

When RZA first brought together the Wu-Tang Clan five years earlier in 1992, they were all hungry and ready to be led. As they became stars they became harder for RZA to lead. The group members who hadn't yet released solo albums were looking at RZA like they'd been skipped over, while the ones who had released solo albums were waiting for RZA to produce the tracks for their second albums. Dirty meant what he said about loyalty—Wu-Tang Clan was his family. But all families argue, and Wu-Tang was no different.

Despite the tour problems, *Wu-Tang Forever* kept selling. On October 15, 1997, it reached quadruple platinum status. It had outsold *Enter the Wu-Tang*. But the group's problems on tour put the question in the minds of their fans: Was Wu-Tang really going to last forever?

DIRTY CAME HOME from the *Wu-Tang Forever* tour in the late fall of 1997. He owed Elektra a second Ol' Dirty Bastard album, but he wasn't in any hurry to start work on it. I think he was kind of lost as to what he wanted to do next with his music. I know Dirty believed the things he said at the Day of Atonement. I know he wanted to change his image and be able to talk to schoolkids and offer them positive messages. Dirty wasn't about promoting negativity, but he was a real, three-dimensional person, conflicted and complicated to the point that in November 1997 he was arrested for attempted assault on Icelene and nonpayment of child support, and in February 1998 *Time* magazine named him Citizen of the Week. Smack in the middle of those two events, *Wu-Tang Forever* was nominated for a Grammy for Best Rap Album.

The album was outselling anything Dirty had done before. The Wu-Wear clothing line was doing $15 million in annual sales. Wu-Tang even had the top-selling comic book in the country. They beat out the X-Men. Dirty and Icelene fought over money when Dirty drove his new Benz to visit his kids at Icelene's place. In the course of the argument she locked him out and he tried to kick down the door. She'd called the cops, so he had a warrant for attempted assault and a warrant for nonpayment of child support, a charge which Brooklyn district attorney Charles Hynes had promised he was going to crack down on—he promised to round up the deadbeat dads. The separation deal between Icelene and Dirty required him to pay $3,000 a month in child support, but he'd only been paying $2,000. Worse, he still owed $35,000 from the previous year. He got arrested when an officer recognized him while he was shopping on Fulton Street in Bed-Stuy, and he was released on bail.

Dirty and I spent our days recording with Popa Wu in his new studio, Brooklyn Sounds. Popa Wu had gotten the studio up and running in the Restoration Plaza on Fulton Street in Bed-Stuy, in the basement of the Billie Holiday Theatre. And that's where I slept. I'd left my baby's mother with the apartment when we split up—she stayed there with the kids and I slept at the studio. Popa Wu had always been Wu-Tang's spiritual advisor, so Dirty and I spent some time talking to him about our troubles, just like Dirty used to do growing up on Putnam Avenue.

Dirty and I needed to spend time around a positive influence, and we found it, as always, in Popa Wu. After years of guiding and advising the Wu-Tang Clan members and doing some guest appearances on Raekwon's and Ghostface's albums, as well as on *Wu-Tang Forever,* Popa Wu had his recording studio up and running and was compiling his own album, *Visions of the 10th Chamber,* to showcase some of the Wu-Tang Clan affiliates who had not yet gotten their moment to shine. He recorded songs for Da Manchuz, the Zu Ninjaz, La the Darkman, and Brooklyn Zu, and some of Dirty's cousins who called themselves the Cuffie Crime Family. Dirty recorded a guest verse, and so did Method Man, but Dirty spent some time just hanging around the studio talking.

At Restoration, Popa Wu was working with Sonny Carson, who was another positive figure for me and Dirty to be around. Carson is maybe best known as the author of *The Education of Sonny Carson,* his 1972 autobiography about his experiences in street gangs and in prison as a young boy. It was made into a film with the same title in 1974—Ghostface sampled it at the beginning and end of his *Ironman* album. But Sonny had left the gangs behind him a long time ago. He'd become a political activist in the sixties and fought against police brutality and for community control of Brooklyn schools. He was sixty-one years old when I met him in '97, and he was still a political activist helping black folks get apartments and repair their houses. His son was a rapper named Professor X, from the group X Clan.

Between Sonny Carson and Popa Wu there was a lot of history in that studio. Me and Dirty were the young ones seeking wisdom about the next phase of our lives. We talked to them about the murders of Tupac and Biggie, and the Day of Atonement and the question of to what degree hip-hop music was to blame for perpetuating violence and death versus to what degree hip-hop was reporting life as it was lived where the artists had grown up, in some of the poorest and most violent neighborhoods in America. And if hip-hop *is* simply a product of its environment, what is it doing to change that environment? What is hip-hop giving back to the community?

These questions were on my mind one morning when I was in the studio helping Popa Wu record. Dirty had just left the studio after recording some tracks with 12 O'Clock. Dirty was on his way home when a little girl started to cross Fulton Street and got hit by a Ford Mustang. She rolled onto the car's hood and bounced right back off. Her mama was screaming, "Where's my baby?"

Four-year-old Maati Lovell was trapped under the car. Everybody was standing there shocked and panicked and Dirty ran over and started yelling, "Come on! Come on! We can lift this car!"

Everybody was still just standing there.

"Come on, if we got to flip this car all the way over to get this girl we can do it. Come on!" People snapped out of their trance and about a dozen brothers helped Dirty lift that car.

Dirty lifted a burning car off a four-year-old girl. In that moment, Dirty was a true hood superhero. It was one of the most heroic things you could see somebody do, especially a rapper who could have just walked past and let somebody else call 911. It wasn't about hip-hop, it wasn't about fame. It was about this little girl under the car who needed help.

Firefighters took the little girl to Kings County Hospital with second-degree burns but nothing life-threatening. Imagine how much worse it could have been. Dirty used a fake name at the hospital so he could come visit her without attracting a lot of attention. He told her parents, "I'm just here to see if the little girl is all right." Maati was too young to know who had saved her life, but her twelve-year-old sister recognized Dirty and the newspapers began to pick up the story. The word didn't really get out about what he'd done for that girl until a few nights later at the Grammy Awards, when Dirty used his moment onstage to say what became one of his most famous lines: "Wu-Tang is for the children."

CHAPTER 11

THE MAN IN THE RED SUIT

Dirty was so excited about the Grammys that he bought a new suit, rented a limo, and bought a bouquet of flowers for his mama. And this was after he found out he'd lost! In 1998, the Grammys still didn't air the award presentation for Best Rap Album. They gave out the rap awards at the same event where they gave out Best Spoken Word Album, Best Polka Album, and Best Album Notes. The winners in these categories had been announced at a smaller, perfunctory event, not the main Grammys ceremony, so when Dirty headed to Radio City Music Hall on February 25, 1998, he already knew Wu-Tang Clan didn't win. Wu-Tang's A&R, Steve Rifkind, even asked him why bother going?

Originally, Dirty hadn't wanted to go to the Grammys. This was his second nomination—*Return to the 36 Chambers* had been nominated in 1995 for Best Rap Album, and he didn't win then either. He went back and forth about making up his mind. On one hand, he thought, fuck a Grammy. Like the rapper Jadakiss said, "Screw your awards. My son can't eat those plaques." Dirty was making money from album sales, and he knew the Grammy awards tended to go to the poppiest rappers, the Will Smiths and the Puff Daddies. But on the other hand, it was still an honor to be nominated, and he would have been thrilled to win. "Are you going or not?" I asked him. "Make up your mind and let me know."

I was excited to be brought along for the ride. I hadn't done any production work on *Wu-Tang Forever,* but Dirty promised that if he went I'd be sitting there next to him at Radio City Music Hall. I'd gone back and forth trying to get in touch with him and get an answer, but he never had one for me, so when the night came I sat at home in Brooklyn with my suit on, waiting for the limo to pick me up.

I was looking at my watch, thinking, Here we go again, this nigga is late as usual. I tried to call Dirty but he didn't pick up. Then I decide, well, okay, he's changed his mind and he didn't go. And the next thing you know I'm looking at the TV, and I see Dirty walk down the red carpet. "Are you fucking kiddin' me?" I said. "This nigga's already at the Grammys? He left me?" I had just gone and bought an outfit for it, so I was sitting there on my couch dressed up, and me and my girl are watching Dirty on TV. You couldn't miss him—he'd showed up in a burgundy suit.

I'd met a girl named Sharlynn and we'd had a baby and moved in together. Just like Patricia before her, she didn't like me being away from home so much, but she understood that was the nature of my job. We watched a few minutes of the red carpet coverage—Sharlynn wanted to see what outfits everybody was wearing and everything—and by the time the red carpet was over I was thinking, Fuck this. If they left me, they left me. So I went into the kitchen to cook some food.

Then a while later Sharlynn starts yelling, "Oh my God, Buddha, come in here quick!"

I thought something had happened to one of my friends or something, but I ran in there and it was Dirty onstage, in his burgundy suit, snatching the microphone. He was up there with Wyclef Jean and Erykah Badu, who were presenting the Song of the Year Grammy to Shawn Colvin, the country singer. Dirty snatched the mic before she even got to speak.

"What the hell is this nigga up to now?" I asked Sharlynn. "Yo, turn up the volume."

Dirty just went up there calm as a motherfucker and sounded so sincere about what he had to say. You could hear the crowd gasping and muttering, like *who is this nigga,* then you hear Dirty say, "Yo, calm down for a minute, everybody. I went and bought this outfit that costed a lot of money today . . . you know, man, 'cause I figured that Wu-Tang was going to win."

And I'm on the couch like, "Yeah, nigga, I bought me a suit too."

"I don't know how y'all see it," Dirty continued, "but when it comes to the children, Wu-Tang is for the children. We teach the children. You know what I mean? Puffy is good, but Wu-Tang is the best. Okay? I want you all to know that this is ODB, and I love y'all. Peace!"

Puffy is good, but Wu-Tang is the best. I felt the same way he felt. Puffy and Bad Boy Records were slick pop rap, him and Mase wearing silver suits all up in the videos. And like Redman said, "I'm too underground to dance with that shiny shit on." I mean, Puffy put Biggie on, but nobody was respecting Puff as a rapper. It was around this same time that Mase had said some shit about Ghostface onstage, and Ghost fucked that nigga up. Mase spent the next six weeks with his broken jaw wired shut. Dirty was a little more peaceful. Dirty got tired of feeling like he was being overlooked, so he set out to make statements and make moves to tell people how he felt, no matter what. He wanted to be a rap artist and an entertainer, and yeah, he wanted to be comical, but he wanted to be a voice that everybody could respect and relate to.

But I was worried for him actually. I was thinking it's this kind of shit right here that's gonna cause the biggest publicity problem for him ever. But as the Grammys cut to commercial, I could hear the reaction. I could hear people in the building I lived in, and outside on the streets, screaming, "Yo, that's my nigga! Dirt's crazy, son!"

Security ushered him off the stage, and the second he got backstage, he called me, asking, "Yo, what are people sayin' in the hood?"

So he's got the president talking about him on television and he's calling me up to find out how people in the hood feel about him. I had to be honest. "Man, I can't walk outside without people saying 'Yo, Buddha, your boy is off the hook!'"

He was like, "Good, that's what I was going for."

And he hung up.

BEFORE SECURITY KICKED Dirty out of Radio City Music Hall that night, they let him explain himself to an MTV News reporter. "Something just jumped into my blood and I was up there," he said. He didn't mean any disrespect to Shawn Colvin by stealing the spotlight from her for a quick minute. There wasn't any real beef between Wu-Tang and Puff Daddy—Puffy had produced the Mariah Carey remix that Dirty was on. Dirty just felt like he should have won that award.

In an interview after the Grammys, Wyclef told reporters, "ODB will be remembered as the legend, the man in the red suit." Dirty turned Wu-Tang's Grammy loss into the biggest story of the night. People look back and don't remember who won that Grammy, but everybody remembers Ol' Dirty Bastard jumping onstage. You see Kanye West do the same thing today and it's played out. He just comes off as bitter and whiny and arrogant, always thinking he deserves more than he got. You see, when Kanye interrupted Taylor Swift at the Grammys, it kind of damaged him for a minute. But when Dirty jumped onstage at the Grammys everybody loved him. That shit Kanye tried to pull was an Ol' Dirty Bastard move. And Dirty's dead and gone. That don't work no more.

And, sure, Dirty walking onto that stage was a bold move, but the Grammys wasn't no publicity stunt. Watch the tape. You can hear the sincerity in Dirty's voice. He was genuinely hurt that he didn't win. He wasn't just doing that shit to get in the newspapers. If anything, the Grammys came at a time in Dirty's life when he was really starting to get sick and tired of cameras being in his face all the time. When we started out, Dirty loved having the camera on him. But by this point in his career, he was fully convinced the government was watching his every move. Look at the way he dodged the reporters after he lifted that car off that little girl, how he signed in at the hospital under a fake name just to visit her and got up out of there before anybody could stop him for a photo or an interview. But at the Grammys he wasn't thinking about the cameras. He . lost and he felt he'd deserved to win.

I let Dirty enjoy his moment, but the next time I saw him I let him have it. "So you had fun at the Grammys, huh?"

"Yeah, Buddha, I mean, I said what I felt I needed to say, you know."

"You have fun on the ride there?"

"Oh, I see what you're getting at. I'll admit it, Buddha. I fucked up and forgot you. But it was a last-minute decision for me to go to the ceremony."

"No, that's bullshit. You knew exactly what you were doing. You knew you were going as soon as you bought that suit."

"Hey, man, I apologized for forgetting you. Why you coming at me like this? You fuckin' stressed out or something?"

That was Dirty's attempt to change the subject, but it worked because I was stressed out. I was stressed and he knew it. I was finishing the mixing on my solo album, *The Prophecy,* plus wrapping up some production for other rappers, and Sharlynn didn't like me being away from home so much. I told her she knew what she was getting into when she met me. She knew I was a musician and it meant long hours in the studio and on tour. But I couldn't be home enough to satisfy her, so I had to buy my way into hoping my girl still loved me. Every time I came home I left money on the table. The electricity was paid, no eviction notice or nothing. But she wanted me home.

"Hell yes, I'm stressed out," I told Dirty.

"Why?"

"Because, man. Sharlynn's spendin' all this fucking money every day, and as if I don't spend all my time working in the studio, she's trying to turn my friends against me, tellin' my friends to tell her when they see me with another girl."

Dirty said, "Yo, I didn't want to say nothing, but she's been calling the studio to make sure you're here."

I'd heard the same thing from another friend of mine. "Yo, your girl told me to watch you." It got to the point where she started calling the cab for me and asked the cabdriver to call back and tell her where they dropped me off.

The driver said, "Yo, man, I respect you. But your girl calling around to keep tabs on you like that, it ain't right. I know her well and I'm cool with her, but I'm gonna always stick with the men, and it ain't right that she's doing you like that."

But this time it was my fault. I fucked up. I had cheated on her and she found out about it. I'd met a girl named Toya on tour down in Florida and I had a baby with her. All my time on the road or in the studio finally caught up with me. There were girls on tour and in the studio every night, and any time I was home with Sharlynn we were fighting. We fought about her suspicions and I ended up doing exactly what she suspected I had been. Our relationship never came back from that. She found out I had a baby with another girl and that was the end of our relationship.

Meanwhile Dirty and Icelene settled their court case. It took three bench warrants, but Dirty paid her $35,000 in back child support. Dirty went back to spending more time with his kids. We'd take a day off from the studio, I'd have fun with my kids and then go pick up Dirty and watch him play with his kids. He took me with him a lot of the time. He knew if he didn't take one of us with him he wouldn't do what he had to do. And he had a lot of kids, so there were a lot of stops, and a lot of me sittin' outside with the car running while he ran upstairs. Sometimes two or three hours would pass, and I'd see the kids running outside, playing in the front yard, and I'd say, "Okay, well, he ain't with the kids no more. He must be fucking."

Dirty was tired of touring, tired of going to the studio, but he never got tired of fucking. Not long after New Year's Day a reporter asked him what were Ol' Dirty Bastard's plans for 1998. It would have made sense to mention *Nigga Please,* the new solo album he was working on. But Dirty said, "Lookin' for new girls to put babies in."

My plan for 1998 was to release my Buddha Monk solo album. I'd finally signed a record deal with Edel America Records. They were a German label, but their American branch was brand-new. I was actually the first hip-hop artist they signed. I took that as a sign we were a good fit. They were young and hungry like I was.

It felt good to hear my song on the radio. I was in an elevator with RZA at Sterling Sound and RZA was singing, "*Wu, gots like come on thru*—yo, that's your song, right? I'm feeling that, son. That's a hit right there. They been playing it on Hot 97."

"Oh, word?"

"Yeah, they been showin' it on *The Box.*"

"Gots Like Come on Thru" became the single off the soundtrack for the movie *The Big Hit,* with Lou Diamond Phillips and Mark Wahlberg. The soundtrack had E-40, 8 Ball, and other bigger artists they could have gave the single, but they used my song for most of the major promotion and played my song behind the credits at the end of the movie.

The *Prophecy* tour took me to Germany, France, Spain, and Italy. I had a meeting with the mayor of London. I went to *Africa.* I got awarded a "Hip-Hop Artist for the Next Millennium" in Africa—the trophy was so heavy that they didn't want to let me take it on the plane to my next show.

"Nah, I'm keeping my award. You'll have to kill me over this. I ain't never won nothing in my life."

CHAPTER 12

BETTER START WEARING BULLETPROOF

I TEACH THE TRUTH TO THE YOUTH
I SAY, HEY, YOUTH, HERE'S THE TRUTH—
YOU BETTER START WEARING BULLETPROOF.

—OL' DIRTY BASTARD, "DAMAGE"

While I was on the rise in Europe, Dirty was on the decline back in Brooklyn. In April 1998 he got into a fight with Icelene and got charged with harassment and endangering the welfare of his children. Then in June he got robbed and shot for the second time. He'd just gotten back from playing a show in California, and he went to his cousin's house in the Brevoort projects. The fucked-up thing is, his sister had warned him she'd heard rumors he was gonna get hit when he came around. But Dirty still parked his SUV outside, so they knew he was there. As much as he'd fucked up the grass out in Jersey driving his goddamn BMW back in the field behind the Gate so nobody knew he was there, he parked his

SUV on the street in the middle of the projects in Brooklyn. And like Dirty always was in Brooklyn, he was there with no bodyguards.

Dirty came from the airport to his cousin's house—he didn't feel like getting off a plane from L.A. and driving straight to Jersey or going and starting a fight with Icelene, so he stopped in to spend the night at his cousin's. He had on a $10,000 chain and he walked straight through the Brevoort projects, past the dudes smoking blunts in front of his cousin's building. His cousin's kids kept running in and out of the house. Dirty kept telling them, "Yo, keep the door locked! I'm in here trying to sleep." He fell asleep in the bedroom, his cousin in the other room with her baby. And he woke up with a gun in his face.

At five in the afternoon, two dudes wearing ski masks slapped Dirty awake and stuck a nine millimeter in his face. They wanted his chain but Dirty said they weren't getting it. Dirty jumped up fast and wrestled with them, then a shot went off. The bullet hit Dirty in the back and exited through his left arm. "Take it!" he screamed. "Take the jewelry. Just don't kill me." The same guy who shot him tried to run out of the house, but the other guy yelled, "You got it? You got the shit?" Then he ran back to the bedroom and snatched Dirty's chain and rings.

Dirty drove himself to St. John's Episcopal Hospital. He walked into the hospital at 5:30 P.M. and he ran out around 2 A.M. The doctors wanted to keep him overnight for observation and to make sure there were no internal injuries. They were particularly concerned about his lungs. But the TV news was on in the hospital room, and when Dirty saw the evening news report that he'd been shot, he knew the police would come looking to question him to find out what happened. And Dirty didn't want to deal with no police. For one thing, he didn't trust the police. But beyond that he didn't want to identify who attacked him because his cousin still had to live in that building. The whole family knew who did it, and Dirty didn't want to make more trouble for his family. Plus, by that time Dirty was convinced the government was after him and trying to kill him and the police were his biggest enemy. Rather than check himself out, Dirty hopped out of bed at 2 A.M., ran out through an emergency exit, set off the alarm, and ran through the parking lot to his Jeep. No underwear on, the hospital gown flapping in the breeze.

He almost didn't make it this time. The bullet had almost caused his lung to collapse. And he felt the effects for years—a couple of times after he thought he'd healed we'd be in the studio and he'd lose his breath. He'd be sitting there losing money 'cause the session was already paid for, but he just couldn't keep his breath.

THREE DAYS AFTER Dirty got shot, he got arrested for stealing a pair of sneakers. It was the Fourth of July, and he was down in Virginia Beach. He stole a $50 pair of sneakers, when he probably had $500 in his pocket. It wouldn't have been a big deal but he skipped his court date to record for this side project he was going to do with Popa Chief from the Zu Ninjaz and 12 O'Clock—they were going to call it D.R.U.G. (Dirty Rotten Underground Grimies). So he skipped court to record new songs.

In July 1998, Dirty was facing the warrant for stealing shoes in Virginia. He'd been robbed and shot on the last day of June, and niggas stole his car from in front of the studio at the end of July. And what did the nigga do? He headed out on tour. Dirty postponed a court date in Brooklyn—and skipped out on *another* one in Virginia—to fly out to Seattle with 12 and Popa Chief. He missed a third court date in Virginia Beach, so they issued a warrant for his arrest. Then in September he was drunk and disorderly at the West Hollywood House of Blues, yelling threats at the bouncers who tossed him out. The LAPD cops arrested him and found he had an outstanding traffic warrant. They set bail at $50,000. And it all started over a $50 pair of shoes.

In November 1998 Dirty got arrested for allegedly threatening Krishana, his baby mama out in California, over child support for the one-year-old baby they had together. She told the cops that he'd threatened to kill her. The cops held him briefly at the Twin Towers Correctional Facility on $500,000 bail, but Krishana went on to drop the charges.

Then things got crazy.

Dirty was paranoid, no question. Getting shot a couple times will do that to a nigga. He didn't trust anybody and he was convinced that the FBI was watching him and the cops were out to get him. As many times as he'd been picked up and locked up in the span of one year, he was starting to make sense. It all came to a head on Martin Luther King Jr. Day 1999. Around 9 P.M. Dirty was driving with his cousin Sixty Second Assassin through Brooklyn in Dirty's Chevy Tahoe. They were headed to their aunt Cheryl Dixon's house. Dirty was on his cell phone, but he kept looking in the rearview mirror. "Yo, Sixty, is that car following us?"

Sixty looked in his passenger side mirror and saw the black car Dirty was talking about. "Nah, man. They just tailgatin' a little bit. Who do you think is gonna be following you?"

"The police? The government?" Dirty replied. "The CIA, the FBI. Any and all of them motherfuckers. They're all out to get me, I'm telling you. I ain't being paranoid. This shit is for real. They got a hit out on me, I'm telling you."

Sixty didn't believe him. They'd been recording at Popa Wu and Sonny Carson's studio at Restoration Plaza and Dirty had been warning them that the government was out to get rappers and silence them, the same shit he'd been talking since Tupac got shot the first time at Quad. "I'm gonna skip the turn here and double back," Dirty said. "See if they keep following."

Dirty and Sixty both kept their eyes on their mirrors, but Sixty was still unconvinced. "If they *are* undercovers, you're just giving them more reason to stay on us, driving in circles like this. Do you even know where you takin' us?" The police report claimed Dirty was driving erratically with his headlights off, but they were following him in an unmarked car so in his mind he was trying to lose whoever was tailing him. Dirty drove a few more blocks and took a left turn. Now Sixty was coming around to his way of thinking. "Shit, they stayed with us when you turned down Dean Street," Sixty said.

The plainclothes officers who pulled Dirty over claimed they'd followed him because he had a headlight out, but all Dirty saw was two dudes in an unmarked car and street clothes forcing his vehicle to the side of the street, then approaching with guns drawn, yelling, "Get out of the car!"

Dirty rolled down his window. He yelled, "Don't shoot, man! It's me. It's Ol' Dirty Bastard!"

"If you don't get out of the car we're gonna blow your damn head off."

Dirty thought this was it for him. He was convinced they were going to kill him. He looked at Sixty. "Man, I'm gonna go."

"No, Dirty, don't do it." Sixty wasn't interested in coming along for no high-speed chase.

At this point the officers claim that Dirty began firing a gun at them, so they returned fire. Once the cops started shooting, Dirty floored it. The cops shot up the Tahoe as it sped away. They hit a tire. They hit Dirty's door. Sixty was screaming, "What the fuck did you do to have the cops shooting at you like this, Dirty? What the fuck you done get me into, man?" But Dirty hadn't done anything. The police reported that Dirty had fired a gun at them, unprovoked and without any known motive, but no weapon was recovered and no shell casings were found at the scene. Paraffin tests later proved Dirty hadn't fired a gun, and neither had Sixty. The only thing Dirty ever had in his hand was his cell phone. The cops approached them with their weapons drawn and opened fire on *them*. When the cops started shooting, Dirty drove straight to the precinct looking for help, but then it hit him: these motherfuckers are *from* the precinct. The police weren't going to give him no kind of help. There were helicopters in the sky looking for his Tahoe. So he drove about a mile to his aunt's house—she ran a boardinghouse up at St. Johns Place and East New York Avenue. Sixty jumped out and ran into the building, but the cops caught Dirty before he made it inside. They had him on the ground with their guns pointed at him. Their aunt Cheryl ran outside and started screaming at the cops. She was afraid they were going to kill Dirty right there.

They caught Sixty inside the boardinghouse. They took him to lockup and tried to convince him that Dirty had turned him in as the shooter. "What the fuck do you mean?" Sixty said. "What shooter? Neither one of us had a gun." Meanwhile another pair of interrogators tried to pull the same shit on Dirty, telling him Sixty had claimed it was Dirty who had the gun. They hoped one of them would turn in the other to save his own ass. "Fuck that shit," Dirty told them. "Ain't nobody shoot but the cops."

The cops shot up his Tahoe, then they charged *Dirty* with attempted murder. Those New York cops needed to get their eyes checked—it wasn't two weeks later when officers from the same Street Crimes Unit that shot at Dirty and Sixty gunned down an unarmed black man because they thought he was holding a gun instead of his wallet.

At the press conference after he was released Dirty said, "I thought the police were good guys, back in the day. Until the motherfuckers started shooting guns and shit. I ain't really into guns. I got a hole in my shirt this big and I don't play that shit." He promised the press he was going to sue the NYPD for as much money as he could get. But he never did. He never pressed charges. Once again, he was afraid of the repercussions, just like when he'd known who shot him at his cousin's house in the Brevoort projects but never turned them in. Dirty was afraid if he sued the cops they would come back at him even worse.

In his mind, the government was using the police to harass him. And he made some sense: the NYPD Street Crimes Unit was not patrolling Brooklyn for broken headlights. The Street Crimes Unit was in Brooklyn looking for guns. The SCU was known as the commandos of the NYPD, an aggressive force who made up 2 percent of the police force but seized 40 percent of the illegal guns. Rumor was, they had an unwritten policy for each officer to seize at least one gun a month. The SCU was a plain-clothes unit developed in 1971 to target crime-ridden neighborhoods and arrest armed felons. For two decades they carried out sting operations posing as everyday citizens out after dark in the wrong neighborhoods. Their motto was "We Own the Night." When Mayor Rudy Giuliani took office in 1994, officers in the SCU said, the mayor and Police Commissioner William Bratton told them to get more aggressive—they were on the streets to hunt armed felons and take their guns. In 1996, some of the SCU officers printed and wore T-shirts with a quote from Ernest Hemingway: "Certainly there is no hunting like the hunting of man, and those who have hunted armed men long enough and liked it, never really care for anything else thereafter." These officers were risking their lives every night seeking out the most dangerous criminals in the most dangerous neighborhoods, but a lot of them had developed the attitude of hunters seeking out prey. Did Dirty fit their profile because he was young, black, and driving after dark with a headlight out, or did they follow him because they knew who he was?

Three days after Dirty's January 21 court appearance, the *New York Post* published a story about a federal investigation of Wu-Tang Clan for running guns between Staten Island and Steubenville, Ohio, where RZA had lived just before he made the first Wu-Tang album in 1993. The police and the ATF claimed the connections went back to RZA's time in Ohio dealing drugs in the early nineties before *Enter the Wu-Tang* came out. The investigation had started with the NYPD, but by this point they had forwarded their findings to the FBI—they wanted to nail Wu-Tang under the RICO laws, the same organized crime laws that apply to the Mafia. The NYPD and FBI were investigating Wu-Tang Clan as gunrunners, and the Street Crimes Unit was charged with seizing illegal guns, so Dirty's claim that the cops were targeting him starts to make more sense.

The idea that Wu-Tang Clan was a criminal organization was an undercurrent on their albums, so you could try to say that Wu-Tang brought some of that shit on themselves. Wu-Tang played up the street criminal image on *Enter the Wu-Tang,* where they wore stocking masks on the album cover and in the videos. Wu-Tang played up the Mafia image on *Wu-Tang Forever,* with all of them taking mafioso names that they called their Wu-Gambino names. Masta Killa was Noodles, U-God was Lucky Hands, and Dirty was Joe Bananas. But Wu-Tang were entertainers. They were performers. You don't catch the FBI keeping files on Al Pacino and Robert De Niro for playing gangsters in movies. Wu-Tang were no more Mafia dons than they were kung-fu masters— just like they borrowed from kung-fu flicks on their first album, they was taking some of the swagger from Mob movies and overlaying their music with it. Just because you got nine niggas and call yourself a clan don't mean you're the Mob. It was just like when we was kids out in Brooklyn—the cops see too many niggas hanging around together, they start calling you a gang.

"They was lying," Dirty said. "I don't own no gun, period. I'd probably whip a nigga's ass if I got to, but as far as pulling guns out on cops, that's not for an entertainer to do to a cop. And that's not for a cop to do to an entertainer."

In 1997, NYPD commissioner Howard Safir had nearly tripled the size of the Street Crimes Unit. What had been a small group of 138 officers trained to do a difficult job became, overnight, a unit of 380 officers sent to the streets to seize firearms.

On February 3, 1999, a Brooklyn grand jury ruled that Ol' Dirty Bastard should not face the charges against him. On February 4, 1999, four newly hired officers from the NYPD's Street Crimes Unit shot and killed Amadou Diallo in the Bronx. The cops fired forty-one bullets and hit Diallo nineteen times. The man was a twenty-three-year-old computer science student, an immigrant from Guinea. And the only thing he had in his hand was his wallet. Only a few hours before the cops murdered Diallo, Dirty was sitting in a press conference beside Miss Cherry and his New York lawyer Peter Frankel. "I'm scared like a motherfucker," he said. "I'm scared because the word *scared* exists. Wu-Tang don't be fucking with nobody, so don't fuck with us. That goes for the FBI, CIA, all y'all motherfuckers. Stay off our backs."

Dirty had been convinced for years that the cops were out to get him. Now they'd shot up his Tahoe and tried to put him in prison for attempted murder. The cops were shooting at unarmed people. When they killed Diallo, that confirmed all Dirty's conspiracy theories. That was all Dirty needed to hear. Dirty had been robbed and shot twice, and the last one had almost killed him. And now the cops were shooting at him too. Would you leave the house without a bulletproof vest?

And wouldn't you know it, it was that bulletproof vest that sent Dirty down the path to prison. There was a new law in California, the land of the "three strikes you're out" law. You probably saw this shit on the news. In 1997 two dudes robbed a Bank of America in North Hollywood. They came in there with a fucking arsenal. They were more heavily armed and more heavily armored than the cops. They were carrying modified weapons that could shoot through the bulletproof vests of the LAPD. I'm talking AR-15 rifles, fully automatic AKMs. The standoff lasted almost an hour. Niggas shot a thousand rounds of ammunition at the cops before the SWAT team came in and shot them dead in the street.

So this new California state law was a reaction to the North Hollywood shootout. They improved the gear and the guns of the cops, and they made it illegal for anyone with a violent felony on his record to wear a bulletproof vest. I guess the rationale was once a felon, always a felon, so when you came back out of the system and went back to robbing banks or whatever, the police wanted to able to take you down with no bulletproof vest in the way of their bullets. The James Guelff Body Armor Act read: "Any person who has been convicted of a violent felony . . . who purchases, owns, or possesses body armor . . . is guilty of a felony, punishable by imprisonment in state prison for 16 months, or two or three years."

The law went into effect January 1, 1999. Dirty got arrested on February 18. He was the first person ever arrested under the new law. That's what got Dirty arrested—wearing a bulletproof vest. When he'd been shot twice and shot *at* who knows how many times? This was the arrest that led to Dirty's court-mandated rehab, which led to prison time. All because of a fucking vest.

The cops pulled him over for a traffic violation a block north of Hollywood Boulevard. He was illegally parked, and when they told him, he was willing to move his car. But he went and parked it illegally again. When the officer asked to see his license, Dirty gave him his passport instead. Dirty didn't have a license, and that was cause enough to get him out of the car to search him. That's when they saw he was wearing a bulletproof vest. They ran his name and found the old charge from the bar fight in Staten Island—the only violent offense on Dirty's record. So they arrested him for wearing a vest with a felony on his record. At the press conference he said, "Hell yeah, I was wearing a vest. I'm scared like a motherfucker. Dirty don't pull no guns on cops. Not sayin' I'm a soft-ass nigga, but I don't want no grandmothers and shit thinking this crazy shit about me. I'm scared like a motherfucker and you got rappers dying and shit and it's in my blood."

His lawyer Peter Frankel said, "Anyone who's been shot as many times as him should be able to protect himself. No one believes that he was wearing a vest to rob banks." He even hired Robert Shapiro, one of the same lawyers who defended O. J. Simpson, and he spent months trying to get the body armor charges dropped, saying the law was unconstitutional. We got the right to bear arms, don't we have the right to wear armor?

Dirty knew it was illegal to wear that vest in Cali. He knew. But he didn't give a fuck. He feared for his life. He wanted to be safe. He was thinking, if I'm here today and I get shot, the police don't know who did it, my life has ended, my career has ended, my kids are starving. I'd rather take the chance and get caught wearing Kevlar and get a little slap on the wrist.

But they didn't give him a slap on the wrist. They locked him up. They made him an example. They were trying to call it his second strike—calling the '92 bar fight the first one—to give him a longer sentence. He was facing hard time.

CHAPTER 13

NIGGA PLEASE

irty was out on bail and he went back to recording while he awaited his court date in California. RZA and Dante Ross knew they had to keep him in the studio to keep him from finding even more trouble. I'm telling you, I had a stabilizing effect on Dirty. I had been the one keeping him focused, inside and outside the studio. You can see the difference in his process of working on his second album *Nigga Please,* when I was touring with my own music and wasn't in the studio as much on a day-to-day level. Dante Ross described Dirty's state of mind to *Vibe* magazine: "He's utterly dysfunctional and lives on the edge. My man's living it. There's no line between art and life with him." RZA told *Rolling Stone,* "It took a while for *Nigga Please* to happen. The main struggle was having Dirty focus on his shit. Dirt was going through so many trials and tribulations: he got arrested, he had personal problems, court dates; he's got a lot of children, a lot of women, a lot of people against him, and he's got a conspiracy in his head. Keeping him pinned down is a struggle."

In 1999, hip-hop was gaining respectability. It had been twenty years since Sugarhill Gang released "Rapper's Delight," rap's first worldwide hit and the song that introduced most people outside of the New York City area to the music. The Rock and Roll Hall of Fame in Cleveland announced that they would open their first hip-hop exhibit—"Roots, Rhymes and Rage"—at the end of the year. They had Slick Rick's throne he sat in at his concerts, Grandmaster Flash's turntables, and the 1989 cease-and-desist letter the FBI sent N.W.A. The exhibit was going to open in Cleveland, then come home to Brooklyn to live permanently at the Brooklyn Museum of Art.

Hip-hop culture was being showcased in museums, but rappers were still being killed. In February 1999 Big L was killed in a drive-by shooting in Harlem—people believe someone was out for revenge on his older brother. Then in March 1999 Freaky Tah from the Lost Boyz was shot point-blank in the back of the head at a Sheraton hotel in Queens. Dirty was more convinced than ever before that there was a conspiracy against rappers. Four young rappers killed within a span of three years was enough to unnerve a man—the question is, was hip-hop to blame for glorifying and perpetuating this kind of violence, or did it reflect the realities of the places these rappers came from? Four rappers—all in their twenties—murdered in three years sounds overwhelming until you look at the number of black men that age killed across the country during that time period, and in particular the number of black men that age killed in Harlem, Queens, and L.A. I spent a lot of 1998 and 1999 overseas, so I came to see how rappers in Europe were raised in a different environment—as much as they based their performance on the American rappers who invented hip-hop, the fear and anger we felt over the murder of rappers just hadn't reached across the Atlantic.

I came home to Brooklyn in the fall of 1999 and went back to work with Dirty in the studio. Things had changed. Dirty had a new manager, Kimbo, and he had these dudes trying to change Dirty's whole style. Kimbo was a dude who had lived in Brooklyn while Dirty was growing up there. They were good friends. But before Kimbo showed up I had been the one doing all Dirty's managing: I'd book shows for him, keep track of his flight times, and everything else. I had been the one going back and forth with Elektra to convey messages to and from Dirty, but once Bo came in he told me, "You don't gotta do all that no more. I'll take care of the business."

"Yo," I said. "I don't need you to tell me shit. I do what the fuck I want to do. Everybody at Elektra already knows me and I'll talk to who I want over there." But then I realized that Dirty knew Kimbo was coming to tell me to back off and he hadn't done anything to stop him, so I backed off and let Kimbo do the managing.

Dirty had a new team for this album. RZA wasn't really doing the bulk of the production on Wu-Tang members' solo albums the way he'd done on their early releases—nine Wu-Tang members with solo careers outside the group was too much music for one man to produce. So RZA produced three of the thirteen songs on *Nigga Please,* and I produced two (RZA got coproduction credit on one of them). Dirty had helped produce the beats for a couple tracks on his first album—"The Stomp" and "Brooklyn Zoo"—but he didn't get involved with the production on *Nigga Please.* He brought in people like the Neptunes and Irv Gotti to produce the rest of the album. "Got Your Money," the single the Neptunes produced, sounded more pop than anything Dirty had done before.

Nigga Please had a different sound and style than *Return to the 36 Chambers.* Dirty wanted to make more of a party album that people could just have fun listening to, but the album had a rock element too. The production is loud and Dirty is screaming his rhymes. The album opens with "I Can't Wait," which is Dirty rapping—faster than I'd ever heard him rap—over the theme song from the old TV cop show *T. J. Hooker.* Dirty came into the studio and ad-libbed that whole song, giving shout-outs to Eskimos and submarines and schoolteachers while a girl screams, "Dirty, you're crazy. I'm crazy about your music. Dirty, you're crazy. You're a fucking nutcase." People can't even figure out some of the lyrics to "You Don't Want to Fuck with Me." Dirty just goes hard, screaming over a horn sample, "I'm the law of the land, got girls under nuh-nugga, I ga-ga-ga-ga got girls under command." He threatens to drop an ambulance on a dude and calls himself "the cunt-breath asshole eater" before he burps into the microphone.

You could tell from the humor on *Nigga Please* that Dirty had been listening to a lot of old Blowfly and Richard Pryor comedy tapes. He was taking it back to the seventies, all the comedians and musicians we listened to as kids. He sampled an old Rudy Ray Moore routine called "Nigga Please," and used footage from Moore's blaxploitation film *Dolemite* in the music video for "Got Your Money." The *Nigga Please* album cover shows Dirty decked out seventies-style in a Donna Summer wig and a Rick James tracksuit. Dirty covered Rick's song "Cold Blooded," bringing back Rick James before Dave Chappelle ever uttered, "I'm Rick James, bitch." Dirty brought in the comedian Chris Rock to guest on "Recognize" and make jokes about how often Dirty got arrested. The album is just funny and fun, but Dirty was serious too. At the start of "Rollin' Wit You" he screams, "My shit ain't corny," and goes on to say, "You white motherfuckers could never take over—you shut the fuck up!" Dirty wanted to call this album *Black Man Is God, White Man Is the Devil*. Can you imagine kids walking into a Sam Goody record store in Iowa City and asking their parents to buy them an album named *Black Man Is God, White Man Is the Devil*? So he settled for *Nigga Please*. Dirty kept the lyrics where he called himself Big Baby Jesus and "the only black God."

The question people were asking was just how serious Dirty was, particularly when it came to the drugs. He covered Billie Holiday's "Good Morning Heartache," her song about her drug addiction. On the title track, "Nigga Please," he said, "I'm immune to all viruses/I get the cocaine. It cleans out my sinuses." Dirty had done cocaine since he became a star, but it hadn't affected him the way I was beginning to see it do. One day I was in Dirty's car with him at a stoplight and the light changed. Dirty just stared straight ahead at the green light and people started blowing their horns. He was just on pause until I said, "Yo, Dirty, the light changed."

"Huh?"

"The light changed. The light's green."

That's when it really hit me that this shit was taking him over.

Icelene realized it too. "It was a problem from the beginning," she told me. "I hated him getting high. I hated who he was around, and the fact that he would get high with the family. That was his get-high circle, his own damn family. He didn't get high with outsiders. But as long as Unique had done drugs, when it came to me, he did not want me around none of that. He didn't want me near it. He would look at me like he would kill me if I even looked at that stuff. Then, it came to the point where he would offer it to me. That's when I said, oh, shit, now I know he's getting really bad."

Dirty started to hide shit. He would hide drugs and money in his dirty clothes. We'd need to go to the studio and he'd run back to the bedroom and rifle through pairs of jeans on the floor. Music critic Steve Huey wrote that as Dirty's life went on it became "difficult for observers to tell whether ODB's wildly erratic behavior was the result of serious drug problems or genuine mental instability . . . The possibility that his continued antics were at least partly the result of conscious image-making disappeared as time wore on." But you can't forget that serious drug problems *create* genuine mental instability, particularly when combined with the effects of having been shot with a gun.

Icelene told me, "Dirty had gotten so bad that when we threw a party for our youngest daughter's fourth birthday, he came to the house and was violent. I was living with our three kids in a house in Jamaica, Queens. Dirty didn't live there with us, but he would come home whenever he felt like it. We had a computer in the house and Dirty and I got into a huge fight because he tried to take the computer and leave with it, but I wouldn't let him take it. He took the damn desktop computer and threw it at me. It hit the wall. His youngest sister, Aisha, was already at the house with me. She was fourteen years old. I screamed for her to call the police, but she wouldn't do it. She was stunned. She didn't know what to do. She was young, and she didn't want her brother to get in trouble, but she didn't want to see him hurt me. I didn't get hurt that day, but my children were right there in the room with us. He could have hit them with the computer. He was endangering them. He was very violent and dangerous. He was losing control. I called the police on him so much that they said, 'Okay, what did he do now?'"

"He was always in trouble because he would always be high," Icelene continued. "He needed help. He wanted help. He would ask me to call drug rehab facilities, but he would never go to the appointments I made. When it was time to go he wouldn't want to go. He was saying he wanted to do right, but then he'd get high and you could not make him get up and follow through. Maybe I wasn't strong enough to deal with him on my own. I just keep wishing I could have changed things. I wish other people had helped me more. Everyone else said, 'He's a grown man, he can deal with it himself.' I couldn't hold him down by myself. He needed an intervention. I wish his family—the Wu-Tang Clan, and his cousins and brothers—could have all gotten together and told him to get off the drugs. But I couldn't make that happen, because a lot of those people were getting high with him. You can't stage an intervention with the people your husband gets high with."

Dirty's records sold platinum, but to this day he's best known for his outbursts and his drug arrests. He was locked up for most of the six months leading up to the release of *Nigga Please*. He went to jail over the bullet-proof vest on March 12, 1999, but made the $115,000 bail and went into an outpatient drug rehab facility. Ten days later he was arrested again—this time he'd double-parked his Range Rover, with no license plates on it, in front of a store in Bushwick, Brooklyn, at 1 A.M. The cops found three vials of crack cocaine in the car. The officer asked him his name and for some reason Dirty gave him RZA's name, Robert Diggs. Problem was, RZA had a suspended license at the time, so when the officer ran the name, Dirty decided he might as well come clean and tell him he's Russell Jones. Which didn't make sense either, because Dirty's license had been suspended seven times.

Two months later, he was arrested again in Brooklyn for driving with no license and no license plates, and the officer found a little weed and a bunch of vials of crack in the car with him. The arresting officer claimed Dirty asked him, "Can you make the drugs disappear? The marijuana charge, I'll take. Make the rocks disappear—the kids look up to me. They listen to my music. I'm a role model. Do the right thing." Miss Cherry told the *New York Post,* "I love my son, but I'm very afraid for him. He's basically a good kid, but he needs to get in a better frame of mind. I'm praying that he gets help before it's too late." A few weeks later Dirty got pulled over again in Queens, driving down Linden Boulevard, running red lights at two in the morning in a Mercedes convertible. Again, it was driving with a suspended license, with drugs in the car: one envelope full of marijuana and twenty vials of crack cocaine.

Dirty went into an inpatient rehab facility. For the terrorist threatening charge he'd caught in California, Judge Marsha Revel sentenced him to a year living at Impact House Drug Rehabilitation out in Pasadena. It was an open facility, so nobody was locked down, but if the court sent you there the facility had to notify them if you left the grounds without a staff member with you. But they was cool there—without even telling the judge they let Dirty fly out to Baltimore to film a video and they let him fly to New York for his court date in Queens. Problem was, Dirty flew back from New York drunk, with a half bottle of liquor in his suitcase. Impact House kicked him out for bringing alcohol back to his room, then they moved him to the L.A. County Jail's Biscaluz Recovery Center. He missed a court date in Brooklyn because he was locked up in L.A.

In the middle of all this chaos, *Nigga Please* was released on September 14, 1999, and debuted at No. 10 on the *Billboard* 200, but Dirty had other shit on his mind. Two different times he'd shown up at the wrong courthouse in California because he'd mixed up the dates he was on trial for wearing body armor and on trial for threatening those bouncers at the House of Blues. He had Robert Shapiro trying to prove that the body armor charges were unconstitutional, but he couldn't get the charges dropped. Dirty ended up pleading no contest and doing his time.

On November 19, 1999, the judge sentenced Dirty to three years' probation and a year in a rehab facility. Dirty was calm about it. In a way I think that after the crazy year he'd just been through, he was looking forward to spending time in rehab just relaxing and getting his thoughts straight. The main thing he was worried about was the parole. He even told the judge he was scared that as soon as he got back home the NYPD would stop him for double-parking or some shit and just look for a reason to lock him up on a parole violation. "They're going to be looking to lock me up. I don't want no officers to be just kicking on me."

"Well," the judge said, "next time you see a cop, don't say 'You can't do shit to me,' and maybe you won't have a problem."

Dirty got Judge Marsha Revel, the same judge who went on to preside over Lindsay Lohan's drunk driving trial years later. First Lindsay missed a court date claiming she lost her passport at the Cannes Film Festival, and she got brought in for skipping out on AA meetings and when her alcohol-monitoring device went off. Judge Revel finally sentenced her to ninety days in jail.

Robert Shapiro tried to get Dirty a release so he could be in the studio with the rest of Wu-Tang to work on their third album *The W,* but the judge wasn't having it. She was already pissed that Impact House had let Dirty out to film a video without asking her permission first, so she didn't want to hear about him needing to record with Wu-Tang or go on tour with them. She said Dirty's problem was his mouth.

He said the cops in New York were out to get him and she told him, "Well, move out of New York."

"But my kids live there," Dirty replied.

Dirty was polite to the judge and everything, even thanked her and said, "Jesus loves you."

"Thanks," she said. "I need all the love I can get."

CHAPTER 14

THE WHOLE WORLD IS AFTER ME

Dirty appeared on only one song on *The W,* which Wu-Tang recorded during 1999 and 2000. He did the hook for "Conditioner," a song featuring GZA and Snoop Dogg, over the phone while he was locked up. The Wu-Tang seemed more splintered than ever before— Dirty was in court-ordered rehab, Ghostface had traveled to Africa and experienced a spiritual awakening, and RZA had converted to Buddhism. Ghost had gone to Benin, West Africa, to seek alternative treatment for his diabetes from a bush doctor recommended by his herbalist in Staten Island. After a few weeks in Africa, Ghost developed a new perspective on hip-hop's promotion of a materialistic lifestyle— "Fuck all this Tommy Hilfiger, Polo, all that shit. They don't give a fuck about none of that in Africa. Everything is the same. But over here, everybody wanna be better than the next one. Nah, it's not like that over there. They might be fucked up moneywise, but trust me, them muthafuckas is happy. They got each other." RZA visited Ghost in Benin and came back saying, "I came to West Africa from the height of wealth and was blessed with a new understanding of poverty."

Since RZA was a young kid he had studied other religions, like the Five Percent teachings encourage, but he found a real place for himself as a Buddhist. He met a monk, Sifu, who defected to New York from the original Shaolin Temple in China. RZA and GZA started to spend a lot of time learning from Sifu. He taught RZA about the spiritual foundations of kung fu. RZA began to practice qigong movement and breathing. He went vegetarian. He became fascinated with the concept of chi, the life force energy. Director Jim Jarmusch hired him to score his martial-arts-focused film *Ghost Dog,* a task which RZA approached with a new spirituality.

While RZA and Ghost underwent spiritual transformations, Dirty committed to his drug rehab program. He wanted to get clean. In November 1999, Dirty was in rehab in California when he got a visit from Detective Derrick Parker, of the NYPD's Gang Intelligence Division, and Christine Howard, an agent with the FBI's Violent Gang Squad. Parker had been involved with the investigations of so many attacks on rappers that people called him the Hip-Hop Cop. He and Agent Howard interviewed Dirty about the robbers who shot him at his cousin's house in Brooklyn. Getting shot at by cops and locked up over a bulletproof vest hadn't exactly made Dirty come around to trusting the cops, so he didn't give them any more details than he'd given the NYPD before, but he told Ms. Howard she was the prettiest FBI agent he'd ever seen.

Detective Parker was convinced there was a connection between all the crimes against rappers and involving rappers. Six weeks after he interviewed Dirty, he personally escorted the actress and singer Jennifer Lopez to police headquarters after her boyfriend Puff Daddy was involved in a shooting at Club New York. Puffy's crew got into an argument with some other dudes in the club and Puffy was accused of pulling out a gun and shooting at the ceiling. His boy Shyne fired three shots and hit some bystanders. Puffy grabbed J. Lo, ran out of the club, jumped into his Lincoln Navigator, and led the police on a high-speed chase out of Times Square before the cops stopped and arrested them a few blocks away. Puffy got a slap on the wrist, but Shyne was sentenced to nine years for attempted murder.

Meanwhile Dirty was making progress on his program in rehab. He was making regular visits to check in with the judge. He had made it to phase two of his treatment, which allowed him supervised day trips out of the facility. The Wu-Tang Clan were finishing their third album, *The W,* so Dirty secured a weekend furlough to record with them. But Dirty was late coming back from one of these trips away from the rehab facility. He convinced himself he was getting back so late that they'd take him straight to prison, so instead of going back he ran off.

Dirty was supposed to spend a full year in Impact House, but on October 21, 2000, with just over two months to go, he ran off. Judge Revel had made clear he'd go to jail if he left Impact House before his treatment was finished. This was his last chance at rehab, and he fucked it up. The court issued a warrant for his arrest, with no chance of bail.

Dirty flew from California to New York and hid out at his mom's place in Brooklyn, but he knew he couldn't stay there long. Ol' Dirty Bastard walking away from rehab was big news. The cops had all these news bulletins on him. He tried to keep moving between Cherry's house and RZA's and different family members and his different baby mamas. He stopped by his older brother Ramsey's house on Thanksgiving and said a few words to the family. Ramsey pulled him on his way out the door and said, "Don't think that you're immortal. Those times that you got shot, you've come out unscathed—well, relatively unscathed, physically—but you can't live like that forever. Don't forget that you have people in the world that love you and care about you."

Dirty kept moving all over New York and was planning to head out to Jersey. He called K-Blunt out in Willingboro and was whispering on the phone, "Yo, I'm gonna need you to come meet me."

His mama got on the phone, saying, "I need you to get up here and come get him, because they gonna kill him." Dirty had her convinced that the cops had some kind of shoot-to-kill order.

K-Blunt was on his way from Willingboro to Brooklyn and Dirty got one of his cousins to take him to the Hammerstein Ballroom. Wu-Tang Clan had an album release show for *The W.* The stage looked like a prison yard—they had barbed wire and everything. Dirty was lurking around onstage, wearing this big orange parka with a fur-trimmed hood. RZA introduced him as a "special guest" midway through the show. He joined the Wu-Tang to perform "Shame on a Nigga."

"Let me let all you niggas know something," he said after the song ended. "You know they had Ol' Dirty Bastard locked down. You know that the whole fuckin' world is after me. You know that I'm still survivin'."

RZA said, "New York, you don't know what y'all are seeing. For the first time in three years, you are seeing the whole Wu-Tang onstage at one time."

"RZA . . . RZA. I can't stay on the stage too long tonight. The cops are after me."

He did "Shimmy Shimmy Ya" and he took off. One of the biggest rappers in the world, with news bulletins on him and everything, made it out of the venue, past security, past the cops, and back into the city without getting caught.

By the time K-Blunt got to the Hammerstein, Dirty was already gone.

BLUNT CAUGHT UP with Dirty up in the Bronx. Blunt picked him up, drove him to Jersey, and hid him out. Nobody knows where Dirty spent that week. People thought RZA had him hidden out someplace, but Dirty was staying with the Zu Ninjaz in Willingboro, New Jersey. I told them niggas, don't let him out the house, but if you'd tell Dirty to stay in he'd go out. Tell him to go out he'd stay in. But Blunt had him hidden in Jersey.

Dirty stayed out in Willingboro for about a week. He was paranoid. He was scared. I'm not gonna say he was in bad shape, because his mind was sharp. He knew where the fuck he was at, and who he was with. Blunt didn't have to force him to get in the car with him. He took him to the crib, he slept. We all wanted to keep him moving so nobody figured out where he was, so Blunt took him to Popa Chief's house. Popa Chief had a crib near the railroad tracks out in Florence-Roebling, New Jersey. It was surrounded by the woods so nobody could really see who was coming in and out of the house. Blunt dropped Dirty off there and they was drinking a little bit. Dirty wanted to have a drink to ease his mind. He stayed there a couple days, just chilling out and relaxing. And sleeping. He slept like half the time he was out there.

Irie, Merdoc, and Shorty Shitstain were all over there. Dirty and them niggas was still in bed one morning when Blunt got a phone call from his man in Philly. Blunt's car was in this auto body shop and they called him to say the car was ready, so Blunt went to wake up Popa Chief because he needed somebody to drive him over to Philly to pick up this car. If they hold your car overnight you're paying extra money. So Blunt woke up Chief. He was telling Chief, "Be quiet, man. Dirty's sleepin'. I don't want to wake him up."

Chief started getting ready to go. Chief said, "Yo, who gonna stay here and babysit Unique?" Irie, Merdoc, and Shitty are all looking at each other like, Yo, it's not gonna be me.

"Nah," Blunt said. "We keepin' him hid. We ain't *babysittin'* him. He's a grown-ass man."

But Popa Chief called it babysitting, and Dirty heard him. They all thought he was asleep. He was snoring and everything.

They heard Dirty scream, "Fuck that. Ain't nobody babysittin' me. What the fuck is you niggas talking about? Fuck that shit. I'm comin' with y'all."

"You're not comin'."

"What you mean, K-Blunt?"

"You're not fucking comin'."

"No, fuck that. I'm coming."

Dirty went to the bathroom. Blunt was yelling at Chief to get going. Merdoc started screaming, "I'm ridin'. I'm ridin'. I'm not staying here with Unique," because now Dirty's awake, and nobody wants to deal with Dirty awake and pissed off.

"Yo," Blunt said, "let's just hurry up and run out the back door before Unique can get out the bathroom. We can just leave his ass."

Blunt and Chief walked out the back door. Blunt looked at his car. Unique was sitting there in the fucking passenger seat of the car.

"Yo, what the fuck is you doing?"

"I'm goin'."

"You are not goin'."

At this time Dirty had just left rehab. He was big as shit. He was like 230 pounds, eating and sittin' in rehab, nothing to do. He already was a big boy before prison but now he was big as shit. "What you gonna do? Fight me?"

"No, Unique, I'm not gonna fight you," Blunt said. "Okay, you want to go, let's go."

Dirty was in the passenger seat. Chief and Merdoc was in the back. Blunt was driving. They went to Philly to pick up the car, but the car wasn't ready. Blunt had ordered some specialty lights and they weren't hooked up right or something. Blunt started to get into it with his man at the auto shop for calling him to come pick up the car when the car wasn't ready. And Dirty started getting paranoid. Blunt was gonna wait for the car. Dirty didn't want to wait. He said, "Fuck this. Take me home. Take me back to Jersey."

"Dirty, just wait here like half an hour. You was the one who wanted to come with us."

"Fuck that. Nah. I don't like this shit. Take me home."

Finally Blunt got tired of arguing with him and said, "Fuck it. Let's go." And they got in the car. The shop was on Washington near Grays Ferry Avenue. Grays Ferry goes straight to the Walt Whitman Bridge to get them home to Jersey. But Dirty said, "Yo, Blunt, I gotta piss."

"Fuck. We'll just wait till we get across the damn bridge. We'll be in Jersey in a minute."

"No. I can't wait, I can't wait."

So Blunt pulled into a McDonald's.

They walked in and instead of heading straight for the bathroom, Dirty said, "Damn, G, I ain't had a fish filet sandwich in a minute."

Blunt said, "Damn. Go to the bathroom. Let me order some food. Just go to the bathroom, and get your ass back in the car. I'm not with all this stopping."

Dirty went to the bathroom. Blunt stood in line to order the food. After a minute he saw Dirty walk past, so he thought he'd gone back to the car. Blunt placed the order and looked over and there was Dirty standing at the counter. Blunt already ordered the food but Dirty's trying to pay for it. "Yo, lemme get the food, Blunt." A couple little chicks in line at McDonald's saw him and were like, "Oh my God, Ol' Dirty Bastard!"

And Dirty put on this real deep voice and said, "Nah, nah, that ain't me. That ain't me."

Blunt said, "What the fuck is you doin'?" He pushed his ass out the door.

Dirty was yelling, "Where's my food? Where's my Filet-O-Fish?"

"Get your ass to the car. I'll get it, man. I'll get it."

The McDonald's workers finally got Blunt his order. He walked out and saw Dirty standing in the drive-through. On his way back to the car he'd done seen some chick, so he was trying to talk to her through her car window.

Blunt was standing there with a McDonald's sack in his hand. "What the fuck is you doing, Unique?"

Chief was back at the car screaming, "Unique, we got the food. Come on!"

"Hold on, hold on. I'ma get her number."

"We got to go! We got to go."

Blunt looked to the right and saw a cop car. He knew that if Dirty saw that cop car he was going to lose it. "Chief, help me get him in the fucking car."

Chief and Blunt grabbed him but here came another cop car. And another cop car. Dirty looked at Blunt and said, "Yo, G, what, you call the police on me, K-Blunt?"

"What the fuck I'm gonna call the police on you for? Let's get out of here!"

Dirty ran but he looked back at the girl in the drive-through. "Yo, Chief, get her number for me!"

They shoved him in the car. He was freaked out. Irie was trying to settle him down. "Chill, chill, they not looking for you—it's McDonald's. The police eat at McDonald's!" Blunt put the car in reverse, and as soon as he started to back up he saw a police car come in trying to block them in. The cop was pointing at him. Blunt turned real quick, swung back toward the drive-through, but a cop car pulled right in front of him on that side too. So he went over the median.

Dirty was hittin' him from the backseat. "Go, go, motherfucker!"

As soon as he pulled into the street, two cop cars blocked him in. There was a helicopter in the sky. The cops had their guns out. Blunt rolled the window down. The cop pulled him out the fucking window. "Who the fuck is that in the car?"

They asked Dirty for ID. Blunt was screaming, "Why you gotta ask my man for ID? I'm the one drivin'. You ain't gotta ask him shit. Take my ID. Give me a ticket."

"It's not goin' down like that," said the cop. "We already know who he is."

"What the fuck do you mean?" Blunt asked. Because what the fuck is his ID gonna say—Ol' Dirty Bastard?

His ID actually said Robert Brown. The lady cop was like, "This ain't you."

"That's me," said Dirty. "Robert Brown."

"Nah, my son got pictures of you all over his fucking wall. This is not you. We know who you are. Just make it easy."

They kept asking Blunt and Irie and Chief. "Come on. Tell us who he is."

"Who the fuck do he say he is? The name he give you is the name he give you."

Now they got Blunt in cuffs. Threw him on the ground. He was finished. Done. They snatched Merdoc and Chief, put cuffs on them. Then they went for Dirty. "Please, man, just get out of the car. Make it easy on all of us."

They put Dirty in the paddy wagon. He was still screaming, "Robert Brown! I'm Robert Brown!"

They took Chief's ID, and he apparently had a warrant in L.A. for some shit. So they took him and put his ass in the paddy wagon. He was in one van, Dirty in another. Blunt and Merdoc were sittin' on the curb. Merdoc was crying, "Why you fucking with us? Leave us alone. Leave us alone. Y'all know who he is! He's Ol' Dirty Bastard. Fuck it. I'll say it. Y'all know who he is. He's Ol' Dirty Bastard. I don't care no more. Please don't kill us!"

Dirty was shaking the van like a goddamn silverback gorilla. The cops told Blunt and them, "Listen, come to the van and tell your man to calm down before we Tase his ass." Blunt stumbled over to him in handcuffs. "Chill, God. Just chill." Dirty finally sat down. He looked at Blunt and he said, "Fuck that. Fuck everybody. Fuck it." And he just sat there in the van and put his head down.

They took him to the station. They took Blunt's ID and made him follow them to the police station, but didn't give him no ticket or nothing. They treated Dirty like he'd assassinated somebody or something.

By the end of the day the cops let Blunt go and he asked, "How did you know we was at that McDonald's?"

"Well, a cashier called the radio station and said she just sold Ol' Dirty Bastard a Filet-O-Fish sandwich."

CHAPTER 15

IN A G BUILDING, TAKIN' ALL TYPES OF MEDICINE

The cops heard it on the radio. They didn't even believe it. They just came to see if it was real. And there Dirty was. The Philly newspaper said he was signing autographs, but he wasn't signing no autographs. He hated that shit. He was trying to talk to some girl in her car.

Blunt drove back to Philly with Irie a few days later for Dirty's court date. As they led him away, Dirty gave them a defeated look and said, "See y'all in a couple of years."

Irie told a newspaper reporter how much Dirty loved it down in Philly and South Jersey. "He wanted to buy a house here and everything. I doubt it now. He ain't going to be buying nothing for a while."

They held Dirty in a Philadelphia jail while California and New York fought over who got to try him first. New York won out, so after about a week in Philly they sent Dirty there to face the charges of cocaine possession in Queens. The prosecutor in the Queens case offered him a plea deal. Dirty had to decide if he wanted to take their deal to cop to possession of a controlled substance and get a two to four year sentence in New York, with two years of that time also fulfilling a two-year sentence for parole violation in California. If he didn't take the deal and he took it to trial, he was risking an eight-year sentence. "His mental health is bad," his lawyer Peter Frankel told the New York *Daily News.* "He's trying to get some mental health counseling, and trying to get some spiritual counseling." Dirty sure looked crazy when he went to court in Queens and was acting a fool, picking his nose, pretending to fall asleep, and asking one of the lawyers if he made her horny. At one point he yelled out, "Sperm donor!" The papers said he was calling that lawyer a sperm donor, but more likely he was offering her his services. As someone who knew Dirty well, I can tell you that to me it looked like Dirty was trying to play up the mental health angle his lawyer was working. The prosecution agreed with me—they called out Dirty's defense for trying to play up a minor abrasion on Dirty's wrist as evidence of a suicide attempt. Peter Frankel had to admit in court on July 18, 2001, that the cut barely broke the skin and had nothing to do with suicide.

Dirty was getting desperate in terms of trying to stay out of prison. He had four open cases in New York: bail jumping and driving with a suspended license in Manhattan, driving with a suspended license with crack cocaine in the car in Brooklyn, driving with a suspended license with crack cocaine in the car in Queens, and violating a restraining order Icelene had on him in Queens. Plus he had bail-jumping charges and two felony charges in L.A.: making terrorist threats at the House of Blues, and wearing that Kevlar vest. He was facing five years in New York and three years and eight months in California.

By pleading guilty to drug possession, Dirty got the bail-jumping charges dropped. He was sentenced to two to four years for drug possession. Still, Dirty got a harsher sentence than some other celebrities arrested for the same things he was. Compare Dirty's arrest record to that of the actor Robert Downey Jr., who was arrested several times during the same few years that Dirty was arrested. Downey got caught with cocaine. Dirty got caught with cocaine. Downey got caught with cocaine and a gun. Dirty got caught with cocaine and a gun. Downey hired O. J. Simpson's lawyer Robert Shapiro. Dirty hired Robert Shapiro. Downey got sent to rehab. Dirty got sent to rehab. Downey got sent to prison. Dirty got sent to prison. Downey was sentenced to three years but served only twelve months. Dirty was sentenced to two to four years and spent about two and a half years in custody.

Dirty got a raw deal. Why you keep throwing him in jail for drugs when you know the nigga ain't sellin' 'em? It wasn't cocaine that fucked Dirty up. He knew he still had to go to work and handle his business. They fucked him up when he went to prison. The judge in Queens sent him for psychiatric evaluation at Kings County Psychiatric Hospital in East Flatbush, Brooklyn, before he was transferred to jail. Now, anybody who grew up in Brooklyn like me and Dirty knows the psychiatric ward at King's County Hospital as "the G Building." If a nigga was acting crazy, you might say, "Man, they need to take his ass to the G Building." And that's where they sent Dirty.

Years earlier, on his song "Brooklyn Zoo," Dirty said, "In a G Building, taking all types of medicine . . ." When I hear that line today it hits me just like when Biggie said you're nobody till somebody kills you, and he said it on a song released a couple weeks after his murder. Well, more than five years after Dirty wrote that rhyme they locked him up in the G Building and fed him all types of medicine. "There's power in the words," Dirty said. We have to be careful what we say because the words may come back to haunt us.

The G Building wasn't no celebrity rehab clinic. The place had a forty-year history of patient abuse. It opened as an insane asylum during World War II, and was still known for overmedicating patients and putting them in straitjackets and restraints, but they still couldn't keep down the violence. Brawls and rapes were everyday occurrences in the G Building. It was low on staff and high on suicide attempts. They finally got in some serious trouble in 2008, when a woman named Esmin Green came to the psychiatric emergency room waiting room and died after waiting almost twenty-four hours to see a doctor. Video surveillance showed her lying facedown on the floor for almost an hour—one guard leaned back in his chair and stared at her, and another one poked her with his foot. Her death caused New York to take a serious look at what had been going on in the G Building. The sixty-page report that got delivered to Mayor Bloomberg documented brawls and sexual abuse and cover-up after cover-up. It was the kind of place Dirty always knew they'd send somebody like him.

Dirty spent two months in the G Building. They prescribed meds that caused him to gain over thirty pounds and become very lethargic. They declared him fit for sentencing in July, then it was on to Kings County Jail to await his court date. While Dirty was in Kings County RZA and Method Man came to visit him. "He got a raw deal," RZA said. "If you're a drug abuser, you need help. And jail is definitely no help for a drug addict. And he's in jail with murderers, killers, rapists—and he's none of those. The only person he ever hurt was himself." Other than RZA and Method Man, no other Wu-Tang members came to visit Dirty in prison. Icelene says RZA always made sure she had money and transportation to get her and her three kids to see Dirty every weekend, but still, he felt abandoned.

His two-album deal with Elektra was finished. A little label called D3 Records cobbled together the recording sessions Dirty had been able to do while he was in and out of rehab and court and released them as *The Trials and Tribulations of Russell Jones*. There were so few new vocals from Dirty that they filled the tracks with guest verses from E-40, C-Murder, Too $hort, Mack 10, and Insane Clown Posse. I'm on a track with Dirty and other Brooklyn Zu members, and a track with just me and Dirty called "Here Comes the Judge," playing off the old Pigmeat Markham song. So there are some good tracks on there. I just wouldn't necessarily call it an Ol' Dirty Bastard album. When a reporter brought the CD with him to interview Dirty in prison, it was the first time Dirty had seen it. He hadn't even seen the cover art or a track listing. He didn't even know the album had been released.

On August 7, 2001, Dirty was transferred from Kings County Jail to the maximum-security Clinton Correctional Facility upstate. They call Clinton Little Siberia. It's the most isolated of the maximum-security prisons in New York State. It's three hundred miles north of New York City, up in cold-ass upstate New York, near the Canadian border. Clinton has history. In the 1890s New York built two hospitals: the Matteawan State Hospital for the Criminally Insane and the Dannemora State Hospital, which was built on the grounds that belong to Clinton today.

Matteawan was for the mentally ill who hadn't done shit wrong, and Dannemora was for inmates shipped over from other state prisons that had declared them insane. In the sixties, a lot of Five Percenters did time there, including Clarence 13X, the dude who founded the Five Percent Nation. From the nineties through today, in terms of hip-hop stars alone, Clinton held Tupac, Maino, Hell Rell, Dirty, and Shyne—the dude who took the weight for that club that got shot up when he was riding with Puff Daddy and Jennifer Lopez. They kept that nigga in there for almost ten years and then they *deported* his ass.

Dirty didn't have it easy in prison. He spent most of his time alone, kept his head down, didn't talk to nobody, and tried not to draw attention to himself. He spent his days going to drug rehab classes and working on earning his GED, and he spent his nights writing lyrics in his cell and watching his back. Imagine believing the FBI, the CIA, and the NYPD were out to get you, and being thrown into a population of violent, fucked-up criminals who all know your name. This was a maximum-security prison, not no celebrity prison. Dirty was in there with hard-core criminals. New York sends its death-row inmates to Clinton. Dirty got hit in the face with a telephone. Some niggas jumped him and broke his leg. But none of the prison officers wanted to help him. It was easier to label him paranoid. What you think happened? He broke his own leg? Other inmates wanted money from him, they wanted to take something from him, or build a reputation as the nigga who beat down Ol' Dirty Bastard. They were threatening his life. They were threatening to set him on fire in his bunk.

To the prison staff Dirty was just that crazy, drug-addict rapper who'd gotten away with shooting at cops and then threatened to sue the fuck out of the NYPD. In an interview he said, "It's not easy for me. I feel like I'm in a spaceship that has just landed here. And when you get out, you realize there's nothin' there at all. I don't know. This is a corrupt facility. There's people in here that are corrupt." We all knew Dirty was a paranoid person, but RZA had no doubt Dirty's life was being threatened by other inmates. He took his cousin's fear for his life to the DA and prison officials, but they disregarded him. "If something happens while ODB is in the custody of these officials," RZA posted to the Wu-Tang Clan's official Website, "his family, his thirteen children, and Wu-Tang will seek full retribution in a civil resolution." In an interview Dirty did with *Vibe* he said, "I think the government is tryin' to set a nigga up. Like Tupac and Biggie Smalls' 'mystery' murders. The government got a lot of ways at gettin' at motherfuckers, man. Them motherfuckers is some sneaky, bitch, punk-ass . . . I love them motherfuckers but they some bitch, punk-ass niggas." A nurse told the reporter Dirty was on medication and in no condition to be interviewed, but the interview got recorded anyway.

The article insinuated that Dirty heard voices in his head. The writer interviewed me for the article, and I told him Dirty was not schizophrenic, but when the article came out it played up the fact that Dirty was calling himself Jesus, as if he did it out of insanity. The thing is, that's what they used to do when they stuck Five Percenters in Dannemora back in the sixties. Any nigga calling himself a god they called insane and delusional and diagnosed him with a God complex, when if you look at the teachings that's just the nigga's religion. Rakim's been calling himself the God MC since the eighties, and Kanye West calls himself Yeezus today.

As Dirty became a celebrity he found that his life was in danger. I just can't accept that everything that he experienced was the result of his own delusions. People—including the cops—really did shoot at him. Other prisoners really did beat him up. I'm not a psychiatrist, but I do know that schizophrenia is overdiagnosed in African Americans, and that the published reports of Dirty being schizophrenic came from people who were not psychiatrists. In 2003 the New York *Daily News* quoted an unnamed source who told them Dirty "was showing signs of schizophrenia. He would look up at the sky and say, 'Yes, I will do what you say,'" but RZA's brother Divine, quoted in that same article, claimed there was no such diagnosis. In 2008 the biographer Jaime Lowe raised the issue with Dirty's manager, who told her, "He's not schizophrenic. The only thing he's crazy about is women." Lowe speculated that Dirty's manager, friends, and relatives were protecting his image by denying he was mentally ill, but if that's the case why are we all so forthcoming about his drug use? In interviews, no one has ever denied Dirty's drug problems, or his girl problems, or all the kids he had.

The idea that we're protecting Dirty's image assumes that being labeled as a sufferer of mental illness would have hurt his career, but rappers have dealt with mental illness in their music before. Scarface of the Geto Boys spent some time in a psychiatric facility as a teenager and wrote about his depression and paranoid delusions in songs like 1991's "Mind Playing Tricks on Me." Notorious B.I.G. wrote "Suicidal Thoughts" in 1994. Kanye West wrote songs about his depression and anger over the death of his mother in 2008, and in 2013 Kid Cudi opened up about the side effects of his prescription antidepressants. Mental illness is not a taboo subject in hip-hop.

In fact, rappers have used speculation about their psychological issues to boost record sales. Kool Keith is called schizophrenic in just about every article written about him since 1992, but Keith told *Complex* magazine he started the rumor himself when he and Ced Gee were doing press in '92 for the Ultramagnetic MCs album *Funk Your Head Up:* "I was tired and was messing around with Ced just to make him laugh. I told this one reporter that I went crazy and was sent to Bellevue mental hospital." That reporter printed the story and other reporters began to reference it. And how did Keith react when he saw reporters begin to describe him as crazy? "I thought, 'Wow, this would be great press!' And the publicists were like, 'This would be great press!' So I just took it and ran with it." So there you have it. It worked for Keith. Plenty of rappers have called themselves schizophrenic, psychotic, insane, or suicidal as a way to brag and boast about how volatile they can be. The term *schizophrenic* gets thrown around a lot in hip-hop, in lyrics by everybody from EPMD to Tupac to Young Jeezy.

I'm not saying Dirty didn't have any problems—he went into prison abusing cocaine and suffering from PTSD from the attacks on his life. But no matter what his diagnosis was, the meds they gave him had a terrible effect on him. The meds changed who he was. The prison doctors prescribed Dirty antipsychotics that made him lethargic and made him gain about thirty-five pounds. He told *New York* magazine he was on Haldol, which is one of the oldest antipsychotic medications. It was developed in 1958, and it's been in use in the U.S. since 1967. Haldol is known to cause such severe side effects in comparison to newer antipsychotics that it's rarely prescribed to patients in private practice, but because it's old it comes cheap, which means it still sees a lot of use in prisons.

The history of Haldol is fucked up. The U.S. Department of Homeland Security injects it into foreign detainees to keep them sedated throughout the process of deportation. In the eighties, it was given to political dissidents sent to psych wards in the Soviet Union. In the sixties and seventies Haldol was promoted as a way to bring inmates in U.S. prisons under control. If a black man arrested in a civil rights demonstration came into prison acting hostile toward police, or paranoid that the prison didn't have his best interests at heart, he could be diagnosed with schizophrenia and given Haldol. A 1974 ad in a psychiatry journal depicted a black dude with a clenched fist under the caption "Assaultive and Belligerent? Cooperation often begins with Haldol."

Haldol is a hard-core antipsychotic prescribed to prevent and treat an inmate's delusional thoughts and psychotic behaviors. Its side effects made Dirty's face expressionless, his walk slow and stiff, and his jaw prone to clench involuntarily. Haldol blocks dopamine receptors, which makes its unintended side effects similar to symptoms seen in Parkinson's disease. It slows down movement and cognitive function. People who came back from visiting Dirty at Clinton described him as looking catatonic. *Vibe* magazine's David Bry, who interviewed Dirty in prison, said he had puffy cheeks, long, jagged fingernails, lots of missing teeth, and half-open eyes. The *Guardian*'s William Shaw said he looked like Jack Nicholson's character Mac McMurphy after he's lobotomized in *One Flew Over the Cuckoo's Nest*. But psychiatric hospitals had stopped lobotomizing patients in the 1970s; they sedated Dirty with medication. He claimed he was so sedated he no longer had the reflexes he needed to protect himself. He said other inmates would punch him when he couldn't even move quick enough to dodge the punch.

Dirty didn't commit a crime that required being sedated. He wasn't belligerent toward the other prisoners, only outspoken about his fears that the other prisoners would attack him. You've still to this day heard none of the prisoners say that Dirty was crazy. This was the story told by the prison staff. The true story won't come out because it would make the system look bad. It's not like today when Lil Wayne goes to jail and the whole world can see. The whole time Wayne was in Rikers in 2010, he had a Website publishing letters he wrote to his fans, describing what he did all day in prison. Dirty didn't have anything like that. They just locked Dirty up and threw away the key.

Icelene took their kids to visit Dirty in Clinton every weekend. "I was working two jobs," she said, "plus the long hours driving back and forth to Clinton on the weekends. For some trips, RZA hired us a driver. Sometimes he would come too. I would bring Dirty money for his commissary. We'd bring him pizza and he'd get to sit and eat with his kids. He didn't really care to see anybody else but he was still sad that people didn't come visit him. He would ask me if I'd seen his friends or his mom. He wanted to get out of there. He wanted me to do something to help him get out, but all I could do was write the prison and threaten to sue if anything happened to my husband. Once he went to Clinton there was nothing I could do but cry. Sometimes we would sit there and cry almost the whole visit. Dirty didn't communicate with anybody at all in prison. He kept to himself. He would act like he was crazy so he would be put places away from the other prisoners, but that act kept him on the meds. On one visit we started to notice he was shaking a lot. I got the name of his medicine to give to RZA and RZA told him to stop taking his medicine. But he wasn't in the position to do that." Dirty knew that acting crazy would get him moved from the general population to Clinton's Assessment and Program Preparation Unit (APPU), a diagnostic special housing unit where they evaluate prisoners for substance abuse counseling and work to ease their transition into the general population.

Clinton also houses one of New York's twelve Office of Mental Health satellite units, which are linked to the Central New York Psychiatric Center. The satellite maintains a separate dorm for prisoners who are psychotic and violent, and an Intermediate Care Program dorm for nonviolent prisoners in mental crisis. A thirty-person staff treats about 450 prisoner-patients, 350 of whom are prescribed psychotropic meds. In 1999, former inmate Anthony Perri won a lawsuit over his treatment at Clinton's OMH. In his decision, District Judge Neal P. McCurn wrote, "The testimony in this case shows that while a smattering of mental health and prison personnel attempted to alleviate plaintiff's torment, the overwhelming majority of those charged with his health care did nothing more than act to exacerbate it." The court found that in Perri's case

Clinton violated "minimally adequate mental health care" services. Later in 1999, in the case of *Ana Luisa Jorge v. The State of New York,* the court again noted deficiencies in the evaluation, treatment, and supervision of prisoners assigned to Clinton's mental health unit.

Dirty arrived at Clinton in 2001, two years after these court decisions were made. He spent eighteen months there. Dirty was in prison when Wu-Tang Clan's 2001 album *Iron Flag* was released. It was the first Wu-Tang album not to include Ol' Dirty Bastard. Dirty was in prison when the September 11, 2001, terrorist attacks happened. He was in there on April 9, 2002, when the NYPD announced it would dismantle the Street Crimes Unit that had shot at Dirty and killed Amadou Diallo, whose mother won a $3 million settlement from the city. Dirty was in there the day before Halloween 2002, when Jam Master Jay from Run DMC was shot to death in his recording studio in Queens. I remember reading something that DMC said about his bandmate Jay. He blamed Jay's murder on the fact that he'd refused to move his studio out of the Jamaica, Queens, neighborhood where he'd grown up, and away from the crime out there. Run DMC is one of the biggest rap groups ever, and Jay was a sought-after producer. He could have had his studio in the most upscale Manhattan neighborhood, or anywhere else in the world he wanted, but just like with Dirty you couldn't keep Jay out of the hood. DMC said Jay put his studio in Queens so he could take the music back to the same people he grew up with, so that they could look to him as an example that said, *Look at me—I made it out. You could do this too.*

Dirty, on the other hand, had made it out of the hood only to end up in prison, where so many of us from our part of Brooklyn end up. Like Jay, Dirty was a rap star who was shot in the neighborhood where he'd grown up. Unlike Jay, he'd survived. The question now was could he survive prison and still have a career left in music. Would prison rehabilitate him or damage him further? Could he come out and still have a life?

CHAPTER 16

ONE MORE CHANCE

In winter of 2002, I was planning a trip to Clinton to see Dirty when I got a call from a young dude named Jarred Weisfeld. He was a production assistant at VH1 and he wanted to get in touch with Dirty about some ideas for some new projects. I was kind of skeptical at first about letting him meet Dirty or meet Dirty's mom. After he started saying some things I liked to hear, though, I put him in contact with Cherry, who was Dirty's manager at the time, and that's how the saga continued. That's how Dirty got to hit the streets and start to do shows all over again. So I talked to Jarred. I introduced him to Cherry. Next thing you know it was all hooked up.

People ask me why Ol' Dirty Bastard would even consider signing on with a twenty-three-year-old white boy who'd just graduated from college and never managed anyone before. You have to understand that Jarred reached out to Dirty when nobody else wanted to touch him. His contract with Elektra had ended. RZA and Wu-Tang weren't seeking out new projects and record deals for him. I didn't see nobody else going to him and asking if he needed a deal when he got home. He was just rotting away in prison. Jarred got Dirty a VH1 show and got him signed with Roc-A-Fella Records, one of the biggest hip-hop labels there was at the time.

Jarred's a cool dude, but he's a character at times, likes to make jokes a lot, and sometimes you ain't in a joking mood and you want to curse him out. He was twenty-three years old, showed up wearing a white dress shirt and tie with a baseball cap. We headed toward Dannemora to try to see Dirty in Clinton. It started snowing real bad, so we pulled off in Albany for the night. Next morning we got breakfast. Jarred's Jewish, so he was used to eating bagels and lox for breakfast. He'd never gone to a place where they made steak and eggs and grits. We ate fast and we drove even faster, but it was slow going with the snow coming down. The storm put us there too late for visiting hours, and they wouldn't let us see Dirty. "Listen," I begged. "We just need to talk to him. He's ODB from Wu-Tang Clan and this is his new manager. We just need a real quick meeting."

"I don't give a fuck who he is. Unless you a lawyer, you ain't getting to see him."

Jarred ended up going back up there with Miss Cherry, and they worked it all out. Jarred would become Dirty's new comanager, along with Cherry. He started working to find him a new record deal and pitch these ideas for reality shows to VH1. His first idea was *ODB on Parole,* which was just cameras following Dirty as he came out of prison and went through the whole process of getting readjusted to society and checking in with his parole officer. He also hooked Dirty up with Spike TV's reality show *Stuck on Dirty,* which filmed a white dude from Queens electronically tethered to Dirty as he went about his daily life. If the dude strayed more than ten feet from Dirty, an alarm went off and he lost money. They filmed it six months before Dirty died, but it's never aired.

That show is one of the reasons that people say Jarred exploited Dirty, but when nobody else wanted to work with Dirty, Jarred got him a million-dollar deal with the Roc. Jarred got him TV shows. When Dirty got released, it was Jarred there at the gates. Jarred was the one who was there, whether or not he brought a VH1 camera crew with him.

Dirty came up for parole in February 2003. He sat in front of the parole board and said he was clean and wanted to stay that way. "My world is full of a lot of temptation," he admitted. "When you got the stardom, you got the ladies all around, you got all kinds of foolish things messing with your head." Before they would consider parole, they sent Dirty from Clinton to the Manhattan Psychiatric Center for evaluation to make sure he was ready to reenter society. They kept him in there for almost three months. So that was two years in prison, three months in the psychiatric center, plus all the time in and out of rehab before he went in. I hadn't seen him in almost three years. The morning of May 1, 2003, Jarred and I met Miss Cherry and Dirty's sisters at Cherry's house in Brooklyn. We were picking up Dirty in style, in a white SUV limo. Damon Dash, CEO of Roc-A-Fella Records, was waiting outside when we got to the Manhattan Psychiatric Center. "He's about to be a member of a new family," Dame said, "so of course his family should be here for him when he comes out." Jarred and Miss Cherry went into the visiting room to bring him out, and Dirty hugged each of them. Then Dirty walked out of the facility in a white T-shirt and jeans, carrying a big blue duffel bag. It took me a second to recognize him. His face was so swollen and his eyes so lifeless that he didn't look like Dirty.

Jarred introduced him to the CEO of his new record label. "ODB, Damon Dash." They shook hands. Roc-A-Fella Records was a hip-hop empire, but looking back we should have seen it beginning to crumble. Dash's business partner, Jay-Z, was nowhere in sight, which had become typical during 2002 and 2003. Jay was preparing for the November 2003 release of *The Black Album,* in which he announced his retirement from music (it didn't last). He was taking a break from the day-to-day operations of the Roc-A-Fella label too, while Dame Dash pushed ahead, signing new artists like Dirty. It was a bold move. People thought Dirty's career was over, but Dash guaranteed the world that Dirty was clean, sober, and sane. He guaranteed that the day after Dirty got out of jail there would be a song on the radio, or he wasn't Damon Dash and this wasn't Roc-A-Fella Records. Before we even got into the limousine Damon handed Dirty the new beat he wanted him to rhyme over.

Dirty climbed into the limo and sat with his arm around his mom. He sang some songs with his sisters and mom. I sat across from them with

Jarred. Miss Cherry laid out the rules for us: "He asks for a drink, the answer's no. He asks for drugs, the answer's no. This is his last chance. If he slips away from us now, we've lost him."

Dirty nodded his head. "I got one more chance. If I mess up, I'm dead."

Dirty put on a black and tan hoodie from his new Dirt McGirt clothing line that Jarred had put together for him in anticipation of his release. We drove to the Rihga Royal Hotel in Manhattan for a press conference, where Dirty officially signed to the Roc. It was Damon Dash, Mariah Carey, Dirty, his family, and me. Damon Dash gave Dirty a platinum Roc-A-Fella chain, just like the one Kanye West holds up at the end of his "Through the Wire" video to announce that he's signed to the Roc. Dirty smiled, when years earlier he would have been screaming and making the crowd go wild. "I'm happy to be here," he said kind of quietly. "I didn't think I was gonna touch no more microphones."

"What's the first thing Ol' Dirty Bastard wants to do?" a reporter asked.

"Give my mother a hug."

He hugged Cherry and posed for some pictures with her and his sisters. Mariah gave him a big kiss and hug and said she was happy he was home. And we walked back to our limousine. We went out to Coney Island and ate oysters and clams with his family. The night ended with me and Dirty singing in the limo on the way back home at 1 A.M. We played the beat Damon Dash had given him and just nodded our heads to it and came up with some ideas for how Dirty should attack it. Dirty said he wanted to work. He was ready to get back into the studio and show people he still had some rhymes left. He freestyled a little bit over it in the limo, planning what he was going to say on the song. Then he woke up the next morning, went to the studio, and recorded his vocals. A couple hours later, Damon Dash had the shit on the radio.

CHAPTER 17

FREE TO BE DIRTY

Icelene says Dirty shut her out after he got out of prison. She was afraid he was going back to his drug scene and didn't want her around to insist he needed some help. But when Dirty came home from prison, he initially moved in with his mother in the house he'd bought her in Park Slope, Brooklyn. She wanted to watch over him, and that's what he knew he needed. "My mom is the only one who can check me," he said. "I have no choice but to mind her." Miss Cherry did the shopping and cooking and cleaning and left Dirty free to relax and readjust to society. I'd come by and chill out, put some beats on and let him write lyrics. Meanwhile his new Roc-A-Fella single had barely hit the radio and people were already complaining he didn't sound like he used to. Some of the other Wu-Tang members were not happy about his new contract with Roc-A-Fella. They felt betrayed that Dirty signed to Roc-A-Fella, which was a slick, major player in the music industry and just didn't fit with how Wu-Tang had started out as the opponents of all that flash and polish. Inspectah Deck compared it to an American signing up to fight for the Iraqis.

Dirty didn't understand why any Wu-Tang Clan members felt he'd betrayed them, because the group had formed a decade earlier already planning to establish solo careers and sign each member to a different record label. By 2003, eight of Wu-Tang's nine members had released at least one solo album, and Masta Killa's solo debut was on the way (he titled it *No Said Date* to make a joke about how long it was taking him). The era of Wu-Tang Clan as a group was over—the fans were more excited to hear the new Ghostface album than they were Wu-Tang Clan. RZA was making a name for himself scoring a new breed of martial arts movies—he'd just worked with Quentin Tarantino to score *Kill Bill*.

Plus, there were arguments over money. RZA didn't want to let Dirty out of his contractual obligations to Wu-Tang Productions so he could record for Roc-A-Fella. RZA was willing to come to Roc-A-Fella headquarters to sit down with Damon Dash and work out an agreement, by which RZA would release Dirty from his contract and in exchange Roc-A-Fella would pay RZA to produce some tracks for Dirty's new album. It was a win-win. RZA was still a businessman, but he was looking out for his cousin too.

RZA had Dirty's back as far as the contract went, but taking care of him fell to me and Miss Cherry. We were there to help Dirty readjust to life on the outside. When she couldn't be home I would come there and bring him some food and see if he needed anything. Cherry gave me a key to the house because Dirty wouldn't open the door for nobody. If you didn't have a key, you wasn't getting in. I'd stop by and bring girls with me because Dirty loved the presence of women. I made sure he was good, but I didn't babysit him. That wasn't what he needed or wanted. I knew if he needed something he'd ask me.

Jarred kept the VH1 cameras focused on Dirty as he worked in the studio, but when Dirty went to the studio alone, nothing would get done. So one day Jarred called me and said, "I need you to come to the studio. Dirty needs to finish this song he's doing with Ludacris." When I got there I understood why he'd called me. Dirty didn't sound anything like himself on the song. He was rapping like some kind of 50 Cent wannabe instead of bringing the originality he was known for. I played it through and just looked at him. "What the fuck is this?"

"What?" Dirty asked. "That's how I rap."

"Delete it."

"What the fuck you mean delete it?"

"Look, man, you're not 50 Cent. You need to be Ol' Dirty Bastard. Niggas don't want to hear no 50 Cent coming out of Ol' Dirty Bastard. You need to give them that Ol' Dirty Bastard style—the yelling, the singing. You sound tired and lifeless on here. Get all the weariness out of your voice." I must have talked some sense into him, because he went back in and redid the verse to sound like Ol' Dirty Bastard and that song wound up coming out hot. But of course he was tired. He'd come out of prison and into the psych hospital, then went straight into the studio. I said he wasn't ready, but he swore he was.

It wasn't only the way he rapped that concerned me. Mentally, Dirty wasn't himself. I wanted him to go home and really take some time off to get his mind right and get himself back into shape before he started spending his days in the studio working. But Roc-A-Fella had paid him an advance to record a new album, so he owed them a new album. Plus, people were asking him to guest on their albums. He did songs with his new Roc-A-Fella labelmates Kanye West and Beanie Sigel. He did a song for the Neptunes, who had produced "Got Your Money" and two other tracks on *Nigga Please.* Dirty felt a lot of pressure, and he still had that prison mentality of waiting to be told where to go when, what time to eat, what time the lights turn out at night. He secured a curfew extension from his parole officer to record the song "Pop Shit" for the Neptunes' album. Dirty showed up with his notebook of rhymes and recorded some verses, but when Pharrell of the Neptunes asked him to add some flavor to the song's intro, Dirty didn't know what to say.

This was Ol' Dirty Bastard, the rapper who was known to never be at a loss for words, the man who used to step into the recording booth and just ad-lib whatever came into his head. When we worked on *Return to the 36 Chambers,* if Dirty wasn't rhyming in the booth he was talking or goofing around, and he wanted us to record *all* of it. Listen to how much talking he does on *Return to the 36,* from the intro track to "Goin' Down," where he just walked up to the microphone and started croaking like a frog for a full minute before he started to rap. Now he didn't know what to say. Dirty actually called Pharrell over to the booth to say, "I'll do it, but I want your touch on it, man. I'm telling you, honestly, I want you to decorate it." The man who had snatched the mic from legends like Biggie and Doug E. Fresh was now ready to turn the whole operation over to Pharrell. When Dirty pressed him to come up with an intro, Pharrell suggested he open the song by singing, "Guess who's home?" and Dirty sang it the way he suggested. His voice sounded good but his heart wasn't in it. After all his time in prison Dirty didn't know what to do anymore but take orders.

It wasn't that he *wanted* to be told what to do. He just didn't know how else to function. He was still taking orders from his parole officer, who stayed on his back to make sure he came home before his 9 P.M. curfew. He and Pharrell made "Pop Shit" in ninety-eight minutes so that Dirty could make curfew. Parole Officer Roach warned him that a curfew violation would either send him back to jail or put him on house arrest and get him strapped with an ankle bracelet so they could make sure he stayed inside. Officer Roach checked up on Dirty, too. He would drop by the house at night to make sure Dirty was home on time and staying clean, and to make clear to Dirty that he was to communicate with him directly. Officer Roach didn't want Jarred or Roc-A-Fella calling with updates. He wanted to hear directly from Dirty. Officer Roach was tough on Dirty, but he was good for him. It scared the shit out of Dirty to have his parole officer drop by Cherry's house like that, but that fear kept him in line.

At the same time, everyone keeping tabs on him put a lot of pressure on Dirty. He had to get special permission from Officer Roach to do a late show at a club, or leave New York for a show. His mom kept her eye on him to make sure Dirty stayed clean. Roc-A-Fella wanted to protect their investment and make sure Dirty wasn't back on drugs and not making music, so Damon Dash hired a bodyguard to stay with Dirty not only to protect him but to make sure he stayed clean and got to the studio. Jarred was doing his job as manager to make sure Dirty met his obligations. Icelene and baby mamas were calling Dirty for their cut of the Roc-A-Fella advance. He wasn't used to being accessible like that, 24/7. He was used to being able to turn off his phone and leave town if people were bothering him. In his mama's house there was nowhere to hide.

The old Dirty was still in there. You could see it six weeks after he came home, at the homecoming show he did with the Brooklyn Zu at this club, Plaid, in Manhattan. *Vice* magazine sponsored the show. Dirty had to ask special permission of Parole Officer Roach to stay out past curfew and play the show. Still, he was nervous about staying out so late—he'd convinced himself that something could go wrong with the paperwork and he'd get sent back to jail for parole violation. He walked out onstage kind of shy and unimposing. "Ladies and gentlemen," I announced, "Dirt McGirt!" The crowd cheered. Dirty said, "I've been locked up for a while so y'all got to excuse me," then he went straight into "Brooklyn Zoo." He was happy to be onstage. He seemed humbled to be back up there with us performing his music. As many shows as he'd skipped out on over the years, Dirty really did love to perform, and that night you could see it on his face.

Jarred kept Dirty busy, got him a gig as a guest photographer for *Playboy,* and got him and RZA a guest appearance on *America's Next Top Model.* VH1 continued filming *(Inside) Out: ODB on Parole,* which was one of the shows Jarred had promised he could bring them. You know how reality shows love to focus on the drama. They showed Dirty fighting with his girl on the phone. They showed RZA and Damon Dash fighting over Dirty's contracts. They showed me and Dirty fighting in the studio over how he wanted to rhyme on a song. One thing you can say about Jarred is that for better or worse he got Dirty back into the eyes of the public. Dirty was being filmed everywhere he went, which was good publicity for a rap star trying to reestablish his fan base, but a bad situation for a man who had spent so many years convinced people were watching his every move.

CHAPTER 18

IF YOU SEE DIRTY, TELL HIM WE LOVE HIM

Miss Cherry was the only one who could really keep Dirty from fucking up. I checked on him, Jarred checked on him, his bodyguard, Jerrome, and Officer Roach checked on him, but it didn't matter. In late fall of 2003, when Cherry left Brooklyn to go on her honeymoon, Dirty disappeared.

He wasn't answering his cell phone, which was nothing new, but the stakes were higher this time. This truly was his last chance. Skipping out on parole meant going back to prison, and none of us thought he'd survive another trip to the pen. I had my people in Brooklyn looking for him, RZA had his people in Staten Island. Jarred and Roc-A-Fella were looking to track him down. Everybody worked as a team and we put a dragnet over Brooklyn and Staten Island.

Some of his boys found him and took him out to stay in a condo in Rockland County, trying to remove him from his element and watch him till his mom came back. He wouldn't tell us where he'd gone or what he'd been doing during the couple days he was out of our sight, but we all assumed the worst. He'd already told us that the hardest part of his parole was staying off drugs. He said drugs were "the only thing that makes me enjoy myself, because life is boring." We tried to tell him of course it's boring—you're a grown man sitting in your mama's house by 9 P.M. every night—but this phase is temporary. It's a transition period to get you readjusted and back to your old self, minus the drugs.

Haldol blocks dopamine, and dopamine regulates mood. On Haldol all Dirty wanted to do was sleep. He realized the drug was affecting him badly, but rather than going to see a psychiatrist to talk about changing his dose or changing to a different medication, he tried to self-medicate with the drugs he was most familiar with—cocaine and crack. Cocaine increases dopamine and intensifies its effects. So when Dirty got high and he felt good for the first time in a long time, he stopped taking his prescription medicine altogether. When Dirty stopped taking Haldol, he started to lose the weight he'd put on, his face shrank back down to its normal size, and he started becoming himself again. But then, with the psychotropic meds gone from his system, his reaction was *I need to get high*. So he stopped the prescription drugs that were curing his hallucinations but leaving him lethargic, and then he went back to doing the drugs like cocaine and crack that were hurting him more than he knew.

Dirty started changing. It was a bad sign when he moved out of Cherry's house and into his own apartment in the Kensington section of Brooklyn. Everything had been going so well at his mom's house, but the moment he moved into his own place it was a nightmare. At first glance you might take it as a good sign, and I made that mistake myself. After all, Dirty was leaving his mom's house and establishing his own residence. But more than anything Dirty wanted some seclusion. With all of us watching him so closely at Cherry's house, he couldn't sneak out to get the drugs. This was the first time he'd lived by himself as a grown man. Not with his mama, not with his wife or his boys or his baby mama. Just by himself. He wanted some time alone, so I figured I'd give him his space. I shouldn't have. That's where I went wrong. I should've been more in his face.

I've heard many people who were close to Dirty tell similar stories. His dad, William, came up from Virginia to see him and Dirty told him to go back home. "Daddy, I don't want you here. I don't want you to see me like this." His dad went back to Virginia and they talked on the phone several times after that, but it was the last time he saw him alive. RZA said Dirty even told him, "I'm dying," but it didn't register as a cry for help. RZA saw Dirty getting high again, and he couldn't see past that to see the suffering that had led him to get high again. We'd been through it before with Dirty, so it was hard to see him back on drugs and just process it as, okay, he needs help.

The help I gave him came in the form of going to his house trying to hide all the drugs so the PO wouldn't lock him up. I loved him. I didn't want to see him go back to prison. All his family members coming around were trying to stop that from happening. Some nights I would be home chilling with my wife, and I would start to worry so much I would have to get out of bed and go to Dirty's place to check on him. One morning I found him high, lying in bed with his kids. Somebody knocked on the door and I had to hide the drugs in the dishwasher behind the pots and pans.

If Dirty wanted drugs he'd find drugs. Jarred didn't know who was giving him what. He would accuse some of the Brooklyn Zu members of getting him drugs, but Dirty could find the crack on his own. When he asked me to go buy it for him, I'd take the money and go around the corner and sit and drink coffee at McDonald's for an hour, then go back to Dirty and say I couldn't find the dude. The dealer called Dirty to say, "Yo, your man never showed up," so I said, "Dirty, that nigga's lying to you. He must be playing games with you. Yo, to tell you the truth I think that nigga was trying to set me up and rob me. You're lucky I came back with your money." That was the kind of things we had to do to defuse him, but if we didn't find it for him he'd find it himself. And onstage you could see the effects.

On October 24, 2003, Ol' Dirty Bastard and the Brooklyn Zu played the Knitting Factory in Manhattan with Dillinger Escape Plan. A lot has been written about this show. The promoters advertised it as the most un-likely bill of the year—Ol' Dirty Bastard six months out of prison, playing on the same stage with this hard-core band of white boys in front of a crowd made up mostly of their fans. Their drummer was a big fan of Dirty's, and when he saw they were signed to the same booking agency he wanted to put together the show. I'll be honest. It wasn't Dirty's best show. Dirty was late to the stage, which was nothing unusual. But the crowd wasn't an Ol' Dirty Bastard crowd. It wasn't even a hip-hop crowd. So they were impatient. Finally, I took the stage with the Brooklyn Zu and by then the crowd was actually hostile. They wanted Ol' Dirty Bastard, not us, but looking around the room I bet not many of those kids could have recited one of ODB's rhymes. He was more of a novelty act for them, and when he finally did come onstage he was dazed, almost. He was out of it. I had to stand next to him and work through a lot of the rhymes with him.

Jarred signed him onto some questionable bills, not only with Dillinger Escape Plan—which was clearly not a good fit—but performing with people like Vanilla Ice and Insane Clown Posse. ICP was known for wearing clown makeup and spraying Faygo soft drinks on their fans at the shows, so a lot of rappers considered them more of a novelty act. And Vanilla Ice had his moment of fame as a one-hit wonder a decade earlier— and he still had his small group of loyal fans—but to a lot of people in hip-hop, he was still best known as the man who sold out hip-hop culture to make a buck. The man whose official bio from his record label claimed he'd grown up in the ghetto and ran with gangs, when none of that shit turned out to be true.

Some of these questionable gigs you could chalk up to Jarred's inexperience. He was fresh out of college and Dirty was the first act he'd ever managed. Dirty was fresh out of prison and best known among promoters for not showing up to his own concerts. By adding him to these other bills, Jarred was able to get Dirty back in front of audiences, whether or not they bought their tickets to see ODB. Dirty was trying to rebuild his music career. It was a stage he had to go through, paying his dues all over again.

On July 12, 2004, I traveled with him to Garrettsville, Ohio, for the fifth annual Gathering of the Juggalos—the fan festival for Insane Clown Posse. They promised not only music but free tattoos, a live freak show, and baby-oil wrestling matches. Vanilla Ice says they were actually throwing stuff at Dirty when he was onstage. It was not Dirty's crowd. But a few days after that festival ended in Ohio, I flew with Dirty to California for a Wu-Tang Clan show, where the fans could not wait to see Ol' Dirty Bastard hit the stage.

Wu-Tang Clan played on July 17, 2004, in San Bernardino, California. We had fifteen thousand people in the crowd, people wearing *ODB for President* T-shirts, but Dirty refused to come out of his hotel room. He was high in his room. Me and his bodyguard, Jerrome, were trying to negotiate between Dirty and RZA and the promoter. RZA had promised the promoter the *entire* Wu-Tang Clan. I wanted Dirty to get out on that stage too, but I wanted him out there on his own terms. I wasn't going to let nobody drag the man out of his room. Dirty finally put on his red Team Roc jersey and let them take him to the stage.

This was the first time since Dirty's surprise appearance at the Hammerstein Ballroom between rehab and prison that a crowd had seen all nine Wu-Tang members onstage together. Nobody thought Dirty was going to show up. A few songs in, the DJ played "Shame on a Nigga" from *Enter the Wu-Tang (36 Chambers)*. Dirty starts that one off, so he walked to the middle of the stage and the spotlight was on him. Then we did "Brooklyn Zoo," with me and Dirty at the front of the stage like old times.

After a couple of his songs Dirty walked to the back of the stage and sat down. The man who was known as one of hip-hop's most energetic performers was taking a rest. At first I couldn't tell if he was exhausted or just finished with music, but when Raekwon did "Ice Cream" I could see Dirty nodding his head to that beat. Same thing when Ghostface did "Cherchez la Ghost" and when Method Man did "Da Rockwilder" and Redman ran onto the stage to join him. Hearing those songs reenergized him and he got back up to perform "Dog Shit" and "Shimmy Shimmy Ya" with me.

At the end of the show, Method Man thanked the crowd, and he reminded them it was a rare event to see the entire Wu-Tang Clan onstage. "Even Ol' Dirty Bastard showed up!"

It was the last Wu-Tang Clan show Dirty ever did.

FOUR MONTHS LATER, on November 12, 2004, Dirty was supposed to be onstage with Wu-Tang Clan for a reunion show in New Jersey. Jarred had him booked the night before for an Ol' Dirty Bastard show in Colorado, so it was already a tight schedule. Jarred had flown Dirty out to Denver to do a solo show in Fort Collins on Wednesday night, then Vail on Thursday night, then hop on a plane back to Jersey to play with Wu-Tang Clan at the Meadowlands on Friday night.

I didn't go to Colorado with him. I was living on Flatbush Avenue, about fifteen blocks from Dirty's place in Kensington, but for those last three weeks we hadn't really seen each other that much. Looking back, I can see that he'd started to push me away and distance himself from me, but at the time I just thought he needed his space. "We gonna change up the team a little bit this time, Buddha," he said. "I'm gonna take Popa Chief, 12, and DJ 2 Evil out west with me. You stay here in Brooklyn and hold shit down. Get at me when I get back." That was the last time we spoke.

Dirty went to see Popa Wu at his place in the Fort Greene Houses. They sat on the couch together and ate some oxtail. "Yo, you coming out there with me?" Dirty asked.

"Of course," said Popa Wu. "If you need me with you, I'm there."

Dirty was supposed to get with Jarred and make sure Jarred bought a ticket for Popa Wu, but it never happened. Popa Wu says the promoters even called him from the West Coast, saying Dirty was out of control and spending his whole check on cocaine, but Popa Wu had no funds to buy a ticket to fly out there (like I said, he was living in the Fort Greene Houses—the *projects*). Dirty didn't end up bringing those of us who knew how to keep him on the right track, and we'll always feel like things might have gone different if we were there. I don't blame the guys who did go out there with him, because what could they have done anyway? You couldn't stop Dirty. If Dirty wanted to do the drugs he'd do the drugs. He knew he had his parole officer and his piss tests waiting for him back in New York. He knew he wasn't even technically supposed to leave the state to go to Colorado to play those shows. But he did it anyway.

The night before he flew out he spent the night at his sister's house in Brooklyn, spending some time with her and especially his mama. She came over and sat with him in the bedroom and he put his head in her lap. He was worn out, he said. He told her it was the last time she was going to see him.

On November 10 in Fort Collins Dirty stumbled off the stage and fucked up his leg, the same leg he'd hurt in prison. He was screaming, "I broke my leg! I just broke my fuckin' knee!" And that was pretty much the end of the show. On to Vail the next day. Dirty rode in a car for three hours, and his injured leg had swollen and stiffened up on the way. They had to put him in a chair on the stage, just a regular office chair with the swivel wheels. He did his songs sitting down that night. But he was still energetic, because while the promoters were trying to get him onto the stage to start the show on time, somebody had brought him some more cocaine backstage. And after the show, instead of getting on the flight he'd booked to make the Wu-Tang Clan concert, he stayed in his hotel room getting fucked up.

The next day, ten thousand people came out to see Wu-Tang Clan at the Meadowlands in New Jersey. The show was billed as the *entire* Wu-Tang Clan. This was not just a reunion show—each of the nine members was going to play a short solo set before the whole Clan hit the stage together. They had Mister Cee, the DJ from Hot 97, come out to welcome the crowd. "This is unprecedented for me too," he said, because even somebody as involved in hip-hop as he was had never before seen the entire Wu-Tang Clan onstage.

U-God played his solo set. Inspectah Deck played his. GZA, Masta Killa, Raekwon, Ghostface, Method Man, then RZA. Then the chants started: "ODB! ODB!" The soundman even played a little piece of "Shimmy Shimmy Ya" as a teaser, then a little piece of "Brooklyn Zoo," but no ODB. The rest of the Clan came out as a group and played their set. Method Man told the crowd, "I have to say it. You all know who's not here. If y'all see Ol' Dirty Bastard, tell him we need him here. His family needs him. If you see Dirty, tell him we love him."

AROUND SIX THE next morning, November 13, 2004, before Dirty finally went to the airport, he wrapped his leg in an Ace bandage, then took the rest of his cocaine, put it in a little plastic bag, and swallowed it.

It was two days before Dirty's thirty-sixth birthday. RZA met him in Brooklyn and took him to 36 Chambers studio in Manhattan. The number 36 was very important to the Wu-Tang. They'd named their studio and their first album 36 Chambers, after the old kung-fu film *The 36th Chamber of Shaolin,* which Dirty, RZA, and GZA had been fans of since they were kids. In the movie, there's a young kung-fu student training at the Shaolin Temple, where the monks instruct him in the thirty-five chambers of Shaolin—they're like thirty-five lessons or classes in kung fu. He learns all thirty-five and goes back to his hometown and teaches the thirty-five styles to the people so they can defend themselves against the government. And that's the thirty-sixth chamber—a new chamber to bring the temple's teachings to everyday people. And that was how Wu-Tang approached their music—they were one lesson ahead of the rest of the rappers, and that was how they were going to take rap back from the record industry and put it in the hands of the people.

In the Five Percent teachings, the number 9 represents Born. Wu-Tang wanted to birth or bring into existence a whole new style of rap. $9 \times 4 = 36$. Wu-Tang was nine rappers with four chambers in each of their hearts, beating strong.

When RZA and Dirty arrived at 36 Chambers studio, Dirty's heart was racing. He was sweating like crazy and complained about being hot. He took off his shirt and asked for some cold water. He kept scratching his head, and his whole body.

The 36 Chambers also represents the thirty-six fatal striking points on the body. This, again, is that Wu-Tang blend of kung-fu movies and Five Percent mathematics—the body has 108 pressure points. Add those three numbers together and they equal nine. But the Wu-Tang monks knew that out of those 108, thirty-six could be deadly. Add three and six together and you get nine as well. The nine Wu-Tang MCs came at you with deadly rhymes.

Dirty was still limping from hurting his leg at the Fort Collins show. He said he was hurting, and someone gave him a Tramadol pain pill.

Dirty was working on tracks for his comeback album for Roc-A-Fella. RZA was working with him some in the studio, along with 12 O'Clock and some other Brooklyn Zu members. Dirty recorded a little, then he sent a limo to pick up his three kids from Icelene's house. His daughter Taniqua was sixteen. Shaquita was thirteen. His son, Barson, was fifteen years old. He said he knew something was going to happen to his father that day. Dirty sat and talked with his kids for a long time. He said he just wanted to look at them.

He sent the kids home, then a couple hours later he lay down on the floor and went to sleep. The niggas from Brooklyn Zu finished recording. Dirty woke up and ate a bowl of cereal but he said he still felt like shit. "Let's get you to a doctor," 12 and them suggested, but Dirty wasn't hearing it. He mistrusted doctors almost as much as he mistrusted the government. When his baby mama Suzie had their son, Dirty wouldn't let them give him any medicine or immunizations. He didn't trust what might be in them needles. He would buy crack on the street but he didn't trust hospitals.

So 12 headed home and Dirty sat on the floor with his shirt off. Somebody brought him some cold water, then he curled up and went back to sleep. This time it was for good. Around 5 P.M. somebody realized he wasn't breathing. They called 911, but when the paramedics arrived they couldn't bring him back. Dirty had a little cocaine in his system and a little more in a bag in his stomach. That's a real coke accident. A dime bag of coke. Not a whole eight ball or anything. A dime bag of coke. But the cocaine combined with the pain pill froze his heart.

The people who were at the studio started making phone calls. RZA made the calls to the Wu-Tang Clan and other extended family. Popa Wu was there quickly. GZA and Ghostface were the first of the Wu-Tang members to arrive. They stood out front of 36 Chambers studio, talking to fans and reporters.

When I got the call I couldn't believe it. They put Miss Cherry on the phone and I knew it was real. "He's smiling, Buddha," she said. "Rusty's laying here smiling."

Barson called Icelene and said, "Daddy . . . Daddy died."

"What?"

"He died in the studio."

"No, he couldn't have," she said. "This can't possibly be happening." She brought Shaquita and Taniqua to the studio. Everything was taped off out front. The cops didn't even want to let Icelene and her kids through the tape. GZA had to say they were Dirty's wife and children. They wouldn't let Barson go to him because he was screaming and crying. Icelene and Taniqua went on the floor trying to make him get up. "This loud, big man laying on the floor, quiet," Icelene said later in an interview. "For once in his life he wasn't saying nothing. My daughter and I started pointing the finger at all his friends at the studio, asking how did you let him get to this point that he laid here and died? Fuck all of you mother-fuckers. I hate all you motherfuckers. He's lying here dead and it's because of you. You let him buy the drugs. You let him do the drugs. You helped him kill himself."

Cherry issued a press release: "This evening, I received a phone call that is every mother's worst dream. My son, Russell Jones, passed away. To the public, he was known as Ol' Dirty Bastard, but to me, he was known as Rusty, the kindest, most generous soul on earth. I appreciate all the support and prayers that I have received. Russell was more than a rapper. He was a loving father, brother, uncle, and most of all, son."

Dirty died on November 13, the same day as the Egyptian god of the dead who'd inspired Dirty to rename himself Osirus. The ancient Egyptians used to commemorate the death of Osiris on November 13, the same day they planted new grain in the ground. It symbolized death and new life and the connection between the two.

In the documentary *Dirty Thoughts,* filmed a few months before he passed, Dirty said, "I guess now it's my time. It's time to move on. It's time for Ol' Dirty Bastard to not exist no more. It's time for a new Ol' Dirty Bastard, you know, a baby Ol' Dirty Bastard . . . and that's just how it is. The government is out to assassinate me and get it over with."

"He really tried to change," Icelene said. "And he was fighting to be a better person. He had a kind heart. You'd have to really know him to know that." He was trying to change, is what you heard everybody say. Jarred said it. Icelene said it. Miss Cherry said it. But whatever force he felt chasing him, whether it was the government or his own demons or whatever it was, he'd felt it closing in on him, and it finally got him.

The funeral was at Brooklyn's Christian Cultural Center on Flatbush Avenue in Canarsie. It's an enormous church. It's so fancy they have a cafeteria in there with an ATM machine, and a big fish tank along the wall. These niggas ain't got a church, they got a mansion and a yacht in this motherfucker.

Miss Cherry was asking, "Where's Buddha? I want to make sure Buddha's okay before we get started." She started rubbing my back and I started to cry. "It's okay if you want to stay back here." She really wanted me to sit up front with her but I just couldn't do it. The band played Mariah Carey's "One Sweet Day" as people were seated. My family and I went inside and I sat in the back. I'd already gone to some of the wake at Miss Cherry's house, but I could not see Dirty in that white suit in his casket. I couldn't bring myself to walk up there.

All the Wu-Tang Clan members were there. RZA gave a eulogy that asked if the process of becoming successful and famous—becoming Ol' Dirty Bastard—overtook Russell Jones. "Sometimes the man makes the name, but sometimes your name makes you. When he was Ason Unique, in my opinion, he was more powerful than when he was ODB. The radiance that he had, the beauty that he had. His whole look was just angelic. As he became Ol' Dirty Bastard, he became more successful, he made a lot more money . . . but he went further away from Ason Unique. As time went on he went more and more away from his own self." In his eulogy, RZA accepted some of the blame for Dirty's death, blaming himself for thinking too much in line with the old hood saying, "He's a grown man. He can do what he wants."

The choir played some of Dirty's instrumentals. A couple dudes danced and sang along halfheartedly to "Shimmy Shimmy Ya." Then they brought down a big screen and showed some of his performances. They showed some with the Wu-Tang Clan, but most of what they showed was some of his last performances, me and Dirty going back and forth on the mic.

And that was it.

Dirty was cremated, which was what Icelene said he'd told her he wanted. The urn was barely placed on the mantel before everybody started scuffling for money, and there wasn't even that much to scuffle for. Royalty checks come in, but when Dirty died his finances were in bad shape, so Icelene isn't sitting on any kind of an Ol' Dirty Bastard gold mine.

Dirty died owing Roc-A-Fella an album, so there wasn't any cash flow from that project. People pieced together some of his last recordings and released them on an "official mixtape," but he didn't have reels and reels of songs waiting to be released. It was more about control between Icelene and Cherry—they both wanted to be the one to say what happened as far as his recordings and his legacy. They wanted to be the one to control the licensing of the songs he'd made. It really drove a wedge between them.

Jarred fought Icelene for payment of his managerial commission, and claimed she was mismanaging Dirty's estate. You had baby mamas coming out of the woodwork—some of them got together to sue Dirty's estate, trying to get their piece and make sure their children were taken care of. Suzie, Cheryl, Krishana, and Belinda all came after money for the babies they had with Dirty, but Icelene insisted it had never been proven that Dirty fathered those kids. She said her three kids were the only kids he had. Dirty didn't have a will, but Jarred said he'd asked him to make sure seven children were taken care of: Barson, Taniqua, Shaquita, Osiris, Allah, Ason, and A'shana. That list didn't account for the full roster of thirteen kids Dirty had told Judge Revel he had.

CHAPTER 19

CHAMBER NUMBER 9, VERSE 32

O n December 24, 2004, six weeks after Dirty died, Damon Dash and Jay-Z met to formally dissolve their partnership in Roc-A-Fella Records. Damon and Jay sold Roc-A-Fella to Def Jam Records. Jay became president and CEO of Def Jam, and Damon formed a new company, Dame Dash Music Group. The Roc-A-Fella artists split between their two former label heads. Kanye West went with Jay-Z. M.O.P. went with Dame Dash. Beanie Sigel went with Dame Dash, but the other members of his State Property group stuck with Jay, which essentially meant the end of the group. Dash took the masters of Dirty's last recordings and promised he'd release his album, *A Son Unique*.

Everyone kind of scattered, like Dirty had been the force anchoring us all where we were. Icelene moved her three kids down to Norcross, Georgia—just outside of Atlanta—in April 2005. "When he died," she told me, "New York wasn't a place for me and my children anymore. It was too quiet. New York for me was my husband. When he died it didn't feel like New York anymore. So I left with my children."

I left New York too. Everything there reminded me of Dirty. I needed to be somewhere else, so I jumped at the first opportunity. A singer named Bluuwise flew me to Switzerland to record a song with her. She grew up in Flint, Michigan, but left behind one of America's most impoverished cities to embark on a career in music abroad. What's it like over there? I'd toured there with Dirty so I'd seen a little bit, but I think Bluuwise described it best: "It is legal to walk down the street with a glass of wine or open bottle of alcohol, but I have never seen—let alone walked past or over—a homeless person, drunk, or drug addict." I was sold. She flew me over to record one verse and I stayed there for almost four years.

I knew *The Prophecy* was a hit album in Europe, but Bluuwise showed me just how popular my album was. The more rappers and singers found out I was living in Switzerland, the more requests I got to record guest verses for their songs. I wound up working with artists from Switzerland, France, and the Netherlands. Even Russia. People who were eleven years old when I started rapping were now eighteen or twenty—they'd bought Wu-Tang's music and were now in the studio making their own albums, asking me to work with them. Being that a German label, Edel Records, had done my album, *The Prophecy,* I had a hold on Europe more than a lot of rappers. I was like, okay, let me just do my thing, do these songs and come back home. But I tell you, it was phenomenal. I loved the rap they were doing. Their beats were harder than the beats in the U.S.

As far as hip-hop in the U.S. was concerned, it felt good to be on the outside looking in. I felt really hurt by the way the music industry had treated me, and my writing wasn't working in New York. Once I moved to Switzerland I started writing beastly rhymes. I didn't have my friends around to distract me with working on their albums or producing songs for them. I was doing one-off sessions and guest verses to support myself financially, but the schedule was light enough that it gave me the time and space to do it all by myself, and focus, and come to realize who Buddha Monk is as an artist. Instead of me giving Dirty and everybody else ideas, I kept them all for myself.

But every show I played I did Ol' Dirty Bastard songs along with my own. I remember being at a KRS-One show in Lausanne, Switzerland, in 2006, and he announced to the crowd, "Yo, somebody told me ODB's brother is in the building. So I'm gonna bring him onstage—Buddha Monk!" I walked onstage and the whole crowd went crazy. KRS shouted, "Everybody say Wu. Tang. Wu. Tang," and everybody put their Ws in the air. KRS stood there and just looked and I did "Shimmy Shimmy Ya" and he did "This Is KRS-One." We murdered that show so bad. It was like throw that on the wall. Frame that moment for history.

I played shows with Ghostface Killah and Redman in Switzerland. I saw Busta Rhymes in Europe too. We played a show together and he said, "Yo, here's my number if you need anything." After all these years we have yet to do a song together, but we had a few drinks and caught up and he asked me, "You still out here in Europe for a couple days? You need any money or anything?"

I recorded guest verses and played shows with Kya Bamba, a Swiss reggae and rap group. I did a guest verse for Djaimin, one of the biggest Swiss DJs and producers. I brought my boy Babyface Fensta and my DJ 2 Evil to Switzerland to record and play shows with me, and I flew back and forth to the U.S. to play shows like the tributes the Brooklyn Zu organized every year on Dirty's birthday, November 15. The Zu Ninjaz were involved. Popa Wu was involved. I still kept in touch with members of the Brooklyn Zu, but we'd never come back together as a group.

Since the time I started recording with Dirty, he and I had both wanted to see Brooklyn Zu release its own album. He'd said on *Yo! MTV Raps* back in 1995 that the Brooklyn Zu album was coming soon. More than a decade had passed and it had never come together. There were just too many excuses. There was so many of us and all of us doing our own projects, spending time with our own families, and Dirty had spent so much time locked up. But one night in the studio in Switzerland in 2007 I convinced myself I could make it happen. I had to, to follow through on the vision me and Dirty had. There was a reason I was supposed to come home to New York. There was a reason I was supposed to be back there. It was time for the Brooklyn Zu.

This would be the first time the whole Zu had gotten together since Dirty died. A lot of them thought it was not going to happen. K-Blunt wasn't even gonna do it until I came and physically got him from Jersey. I showed up at his house in Willingboro and said, "Blunt, I need you to help me make this album happen." Meanwhile, some of the other Zu members were telling him not to forget this was not a Zu Ninjaz album, telling him to fall back and let the group shine as a group. This was what my world was about. I had to think fast on my toes for myself and for a whole army. The army is vast. I kept the Brooklyn Zu together. When it was time to get them niggas in the studio it was me and Blunt cussin' them niggas out.

We got a deal with a label and they sent us down to Orlando, Florida, to record. They signed us as Ol' Dirty Bastard's Brooklyn Zu, which led people to criticize us for putting Dirty's name on an album he didn't even appear on. But our whole movement was Dirty. We drew strength from his name, but his name lived on through us as well. We were out there keeping his name alive. The Zu was his cousins, his boys, the people who loved him most in the world. The same niggas who was rhyming with him in Brooklyn when we was teenagers. The Zu was Dirty's cousins 12 O'Clock and Merdoc and Shorty Shitstain who'd gotten harassed by the cops with him on the corner of Putnam and Franklin. It was the Zu Ninjaz, who'd hidden him out in Willingboro when he was wanted by the police. Popa Chief, who'd been with him when he got arrested for stealing those sneakers in Virginia Beach, and went with him for his last shows in Colorado. And me, who'd been by his side onstage and in the studio since the beginning.

I got the army together and we went down to Orlando to record. The album took two months to make, but we stayed down there for five months and hit up the 7-Eleven for food and libations. We stole beer, licorice, deodorant, gas, bread, Coke. American cheese and mayonnaise and bread. Tomatoes. We cleared 'em out. We took all the Kool-Aid, the sugar, the Miracle Whip. We came back with the beef franks and Blunt said, "Damn, ain't y'all steal nothing vegetarian?"

"Well, man up, motherfucker," I told him. "Get you some baggy pants on and let's go to the store." I took Blunt back in and stole some cheese. I stuffed two salad packs in my pants. We looked at the dude stocking the milk and the juice and I asked, "Yo, man, are you sure these milks is good? Do you got any fresher ones in the back?" And when he came back we were gone and so was everything out of the freezer.

By the end of 2007 we finished the album: *Chamber Number 9, Verse 32*. It was hot. *XXL* magazine said it was what a new Wu-Tang Clan album should sound like. The Wu-Tang members supported us, too. RZA was a guest on our album. Masta Killa was on it. GZA was on it. Some reviewers complained that Dirty's face was on the album cover when he wasn't on the album, but they didn't understand what Dirty had meant to us. Dirty was our leader. Without Dirty there wouldn't have been a Brooklyn Zu. Dirty had told me that my job was to keep the Brooklyn Zu together, which was not an easy fucking task. I'd gotten us through making the album, but we couldn't keep it together on tour.

The Zu Ninjaz was some amped-up niggas, so they was saying, "Come on. Let's go. We gotta go." But they always wanted to leave too early. So now I got one team over here ready to leave at 9:45, and I got the other team over there, and I can't find the first one of them niggas. So if the schedule said the show starts at ten, I'd send the Zu Ninjaz over at ten to cover while I scrambled to find the rest of the Brooklyn Zu before the club's curfew. Sometimes by the time we got to the club we only had ten minutes to perform because it took me that long to find everybody, and beat traffic, and beat tickets, and make sure nobody was smoking weed in the car when the cops pulled us over, and be the sanest one while everybody else was drinking too much. I was holding thousands of dollars on me, making sure the music got to the DJ, going back and forth with the promoters, and making sure we covered security.

Once the tour fell apart, I went home to Brooklyn and got on public assistance. That's right. I traveled the globe with Dirty, and I ended up back in Brooklyn on food stamps. I'd been having some health problems for a while, and the doctors diagnosed me with a heart condition. All them hours I put in with my music caused me congestive heart failure. Stress at the studio, stress on tour. Stress over women. There's no health care for people in the music business. Elektra never set me up with no pension plan for all them hours I spent in the studio. The music that makes money is a young man's game, and when you get older and you get sick, well, that's all on you.

I was forty years old. I'd been rhyming and producing for more than half my life. Some of the biggest-selling tracks I worked on send me no royalties because my name got left off the credits. For the sake of my health, I needed to take a break from all the touring I'd been doing, and just rest and take it easy for a while. But public assistance only takes you so far, so I had my hustle too. I choose not to go back to selling weed because I don't want my kids seeing me do that, but I listen for what the streets need and I get the dollars in return.

I started hustling movies. I was selling bootleg DVDs and I was killing it. I'd go to pick up my public assistance and sell movies to the welfare workers. Walk up in there with a box full of movies and walk out with six hundred in my pocket, plus the welfare check.

"We ain't never had movies this good, Buddha. Everybody else's shit be burning up my DVD player and shit. Yours play good."

That was my thing. Whatever I'm doing I put myself into it. My craft is incredible 'cause I was taught by my brother, by Dirty, by RZA, by Popa Wu. Anything that we did or we wanted to do, that's the science of the Buddha Monk, to bring things into existence. For me to have that name I had to carry out that order. I'm not gonna put out this record and the vocals sound muffled and distorted. When I hear a song sound that way I be thinking the shit is not close to jazzy, the vocal and the music don't sound like jazz or R&B. Damn, I wish I had been there when they made it. I want it to sound like I'm in heaven when I hear this track.

Today I'm working with a new crew, the Zu Bulliez. My right-hand men these days are Judah Priest, Barack O. Dama, and Senior Brown, but the Zu Bulliez crew is massive. We got T. Leo, Wasabi Fresh aka King Fresh, Bruiz, DJ Ghetto (he used to DJ for RZA), Matt Bastardo, and many others. I've never stopped making music, but I've finally figured out how to balance my career and my passion for music with my family life. In April 2011, I moved from Brooklyn to Worcester, Massachusetts. I was kidnapped by a very lovely lady, Atlantis Price. She convinced me to move up to her hometown and we've been together for three years now. Atlantis hosts a radio show called *Indie Corna* on the Nichols College radio station, every Sunday night from ten to eleven. She is a Worcester native, the daughter of the jazz musician Elwood Price and the social activist Elizabeth "Betty" Price. Betty passed away in 1992, but her legacy lives on. She was the first black woman elected to the school committee in Worcester, she helped to rewrite the town charter, and back in the sixties—with participation from Worcester native Abbie Hoffman—she helped found Prospect House, an African American community center.

Atlantis and I found a place big enough that I could set up a recording studio in a spare bedroom. Senior Brown from the Zu Bulliez moved in with his five-year-old son, my godson Jyzayah. I went to church for the christening and went through the ritual to become the godfather. We made him a tiny Buddha Monk shirt and everything. The fifth member of our household is my sixteen-year-old nephew, Wasabi Fresh aka King Fresh. He's not my nephew by blood but I call him my nephew because we have the same tendencies and our attitudes are the same. When I met him he was a little snotty nose kid, and he used to come over to my house and play video games with Senior Brown and me. When his mom's place got infested with bedbugs and she had to move, he still had schooling to do in Worcester, so she asked me, "Could he stay with you?"

He finished the school year living with me and passed with flying colors. That summer he moved to Boston with his family, but when we talked on the phone I could tell he was dissatisfied with where he was living, so I asked him to come back here for a weekend. That's when Atlantis and I figured out he'd never enrolled in school in Boston. School had been in for a month and he hadn't gone once. So the next morning I took him to Dorothy High in Worcester and I got him enrolled. He's been living with us for two years now. We make it work as a family. Without them I don't know what I would do. They play a big part in my life. I love them. They mean the world to me. Atlantis Price came into my life and helped me become a better man and learn how to treat a beautiful woman. My nephew came into my life and showed me what it takes to be responsible for a child.

As for my Wu-Tang family, the Clan soldiered on without Dirty, and they're still fighting their same old battles within the group. In December 2007, when they released *8 Diagrams,* Ghostface complained that the album came out too close to his solo album *Big Doe Rehab,* and Raekwon said he wasn't happy with RZA's new style of production, which he thought was too polished and used too many guitars. Rae went so far as to announce he was planning to record a Wu-Tang Clan album featuring all the members *except* RZA. Ghost and Rae went back and forth with

RZA a little bit in the press, but in the end they came back together and got onto the stage. Not that RZA didn't respect the opinions of the rest of the group, but he said he truly missed the critical ear Dirty had always lent him in the studio: "Dirty was real, he always gave me the real truth. If Dirty had said this album was weak, I would have really had to reevaluate it. Dirty is missed because of the realism he would have given you: his spirit, his personality. But his spirit rubbed off on us. You can hear it on the record."

Still, money remains an issue. Raekwon complained in 2008 that he wasn't paid for some of the shows Wu-Tang played for the *8 Diagrams* tour. U-God sued RZA's Wu-Tang Music Group for $170,000 for unpaid album advances, concert appearances, and publishing royalties. Cappadonna complained to the press that he hadn't been paid some of his royalties. This is the kind of squabbling that broke up N.W.A, the world's most dangerous crew. This is the music business. I haven't gotten credit for some of the songs I produced and the work that I did in the studio. My crew tells me, "Fuck this shit, Buddha. You can't keep letting niggas get away with this." And not even just stealing credit—actually stealing the music. Motherfuckers broke in my Suburban and stole my music. I lost music in storage. I have reels in Sonny Carson's vault at Brooklyn Sounds studio in Restoration Plaza—niggas think it belongs to Dirty 'cause it says Chung King on it, but they are all my reels. They're holding albums I produced for Da Manchuz and Zu Ninjaz. The studio is trying to say Dirty owed them money so they're holding music I made.

Dirty's son Barson is facing a similar situation with Damon Dash, who still owns the rights to the unreleased music Dirty recorded for Roc-A-Fella before his death. Def Jam bought Roc-A-Fella only weeks after Dirty died, and Dame Dash took the recordings with him to his new company, Dame Dash Music Group, which has since folded. "Tell Dame Dash that I'm looking for him and I want those masters," Barson said on a radio interview in 2013. "Why we gotta go through the courts when we could do this man-to-man? We need to build about it and let's get this thing right. He got my father's songs and I want them back . . . He had a nice size album and I want it."

Other people feel cheated too, I'm sure. I'm not hating on nobody and

I'm not mad at nobody but I'm still hurt by this industry that I haven't gotten credit for what I did for Dirty. I've been there since day one, since before the first Wu-Tang Clan album. My family is proud of my success. My kids feel like I've been cheated out of a lot of things. They know that I'm not a one-hit wonder. I'm still out there doing it. I'm still touring and making music. My family loves what I've done with my music. My mother's one of the happiest people in the world. She just feels hurt because I didn't get recognition for a lot of things I did. She feels I'm not getting back the same love I put out.

Dirty's been gone for ten years now, but we're making sure he is not forgotten. Dirty's cousin Raison the Zu Keeper made a documentary about Dirty and commissioned the ODB mural at the corner of Putnam and Franklin in Bed-Stuy. And that ain't the only mural. *Ego Trip* magazine posted pictures of thirty different Ol' Dirty Bastard murals from all around the world, from Montpellier, France, to Le Gosier, Guadeloupe.

In September 2013, Wu-Tang Clan paid its own tribute by performing with a hologram of Ol' Dirty Bastard at Rock the Bells, the same festival where Dirty performed with the group for the last time. It was a momentous occasion, but I can't say it went off without a hitch. The plan was for Dirty's hologram to join Wu-Tang at the end of the concert, so Wu-Tang came out and began to perform—minus Ghostface and Raekwon, who didn't show up. The venue's sound was so bad that the music cut out entirely about ten minutes into Wu-Tang's set. Method Man's mic was still working, so he did a freestyle rhyme a cappella and even told a few jokes to fill the dead air. Wu-Tang was standing onstage for almost five minutes without sound. Meth finally said, "Two more minutes and I'm walking out of here, hologram or not." Another five minutes passed, and the promoter decided to just fast-forward to Dirty's part. The visual team got Dirty's hologram ready while the sound team finally got the problems fixed on their end. Onstage, Meth called out the promoters for fucking up the show, and RZA tried to defend them. The show went off, but with a few snags.

Icelene had some problems with the promoters as well. Initially, the promoters had cleared their plans for the hologram with RZA and Miss Cherry but not with Icelene, who as the widow remains the administrator of Dirty's estate. Icelene was upset not because she was opposed to the hologram, but because she wanted to be consulted. As the estate administrator, she wanted to be a part of the event. In the end, the promoters worked it out with her and not only had her on hand for the hologram performance, but put Barson onstage with his daddy. Barson calls himself Boy Jones or the Young Dirty Bastard. He's released songs on his own and plays his own shows, plus he's toured with the Wu-Tang Clan—they bring him onstage when they play his dad's songs. So at Rock the Bells in 2013, twenty-four-year-old Barson performed with Wu-Tang alongside a hologram of his father. They did "Shimmy Shimmy Ya" together.

Barson had his hair done straight up in braids the way Dirty had his done on his infamous welfare card, and how Barson had his hair done on that infamous day when, as a six-year-old, he went with Dirty to pick up that welfare check. Still, Barson said in an interview after the concert that he wasn't trying to become a copy of his dad or fall victim to the same lifestyle he led: "I'd rather be sober and continue his legacy," he said. "I do the opposite of everything he did. I don't smoke, don't drink, and I'm learning how to have less babies." But the apple doesn't fall far from the tree. Barson continued, "We always had food stamps. If food stamps weren't there, I couldn't be rapping. I gotta provide for my family. Babies gotta eat, G. It's real. That's how I'm standing, [how] my mama fed me. We need food stamps, government! Fuck Republicans."

Yes, Dirty has grandkids. He would have loved to be here to see that! Dirty proclaimed at the 1998 Grammys that Wu-Tang Clan was for the children. In 2014, a lot of those children are grown. Maati Lovell, the little girl Dirty rescued from under the car, is a sophomore studying fashion at Lincoln University. Ghostface's son Sun God raps. GZA's son Young Justice raps. U-God's son Dante—the one who was shot in crossfire when he was two years old—proved the doctors wrong and fought for years in physical therapy for his spinal injury until he relearned to walk. Today he's rapping onstage as INTell and taking college classes full time. Dirty would have been one of the old folks now, like me.

I still keep in touch with Dirty's family. I don't see Icelene and their kids very often because they live down in Georgia, where Icelene recently went back to school to get her medical assistant degree. "It was real hard to focus and go to school after so many years away from it," she told me. "But I graduated in 2012. My kids are proud of me, and it gave me something to focus on when things aren't going well. Barson's into his music. Every day he's on somebody's show or somebody's song. Every day he's out in the club. He can't sit still and not do something." Taniqua is her brother's road manager, and Shaquita has created a line of Ol' Dirty Bastard T-shirts and merchandise that she sells at Barson's shows and when he performs at Wu-Tang shows. She also works as a cashier at Walmart. "What are me and the kids doing today?" asked Icelene, repeating the question I'd asked her. "Well, if we had some money, we'd go to Footprints Café to get Jamaican food."

I still visit Dirty's mother, Miss Cherry, regularly. When Wu-Tang has a show in New York, RZA sometimes brings her onto the stage, so she can feel the love the city still has for her son. She's lost two children now. Dirty's sister Dionne died of pancreatic cancer on November 13, 2011—eight years to the day after Dirty died. Believe me, Dirty would have seen a conspiracy in that!

As many times as Dirty told us the FBI was watching him, now the world has seen the proof. His FBI files were finally released in 2012, thanks to the Freedom of Information Act. It turns out the NYPD considered the Wu-Tang Clan a gang. They claimed they were drug runners connected to carjackings and murders and all types of shit. And once the NYPD had put together a file on Wu-Tang, they passed their file along to the ATF and the FBI. So when Dirty put that line in a song—"FBI, don't you be watching me"—the FBI really was watching him.

Dirty's FBI file also showed that the Bureau and the NYPD had been seriously following a lead on the dudes who'd robbed and shot Dirty at his cousin's house in Brooklyn: "The subjects were current or former industry insiders who had banded together to commit the robberies." Detective Derrick Parker had been following this lead since 1999, when he'd traveled to California to interview Dirty while he was in rehab, and he'd finally got a confession from a suspect. The NYPD had arrested a dude on another robbery charge and he admitted his involvement in Dirty's robbery and shooting—"I robbed that man," he said. "We needed the money." He was part of a group called the Brevoort G-Squad—Detective

Parker claims in his book *Notorious C.O.P.: The Inside Story of the Tupac, Biggie, and Jam Master Jay Investigations from the NYPD's First "Hip-Hop Cop"* that they were responsible for robbing not only Dirty, but Foxy Brown, Busta Rhymes, and Memphis Bleek—*and* firing shots at DJ Clue.

With niggas shooting at rappers, Dirty had always insisted it was his right to protect himself by wearing a bulletproof vest. Dirty's lawyer argued at his trial that the law was unconstitutional. In 2010, the state of California finally agreed with him. Almost twelve years after Dirty was arrested, California repealed the James Guelff Body Armor Act that had outlawed vests for convicted felons. The Second District Court of Appeal in Los Angeles ruled the law "unconstitutionally void for vagueness because it does not provide fair notice of which protective body vests constitute the body armor made illegal by the statute." That body armor charge truly complicated Dirty's court case—his other charges were mostly for drug possession. Without that law on the books, his trial and sentencing could have gone differently.

If I could go back and change anything, I would have tried to be there at certain times when they tried to lock Dirty up. I would've paid more attention to the drug use. The media presents it like Dirty's drug addiction killed him, but I still say it was an accident. Everybody in this industry has done drugs, and Dirty was no exception, but he just happened to not think straight and take that painkiller that reacted with the cocaine he had in his system. He caught a bad shot.

I never forget about Dirty. Every time I do a show I see the love that people have for him around the world. Dirty was proud of getting nominated for a Grammy, going gold on his albums. Proud of his mother, his grandmother, and his father being alive to see him succeed. He was proud of people around the world accepting him and his music and his way of doing music, of there being no father to his style. You didn't know what the hell was gonna come out of his mouth. He realized that people loved him, that he could say *nothing* and people would still love him. Niggas would stop listening to the rap just to hear him say dumb shit. You'd be like, wow. Wow.

Back when Dirty's first album came out we did a show in Miami. I knew this girl I had grown up with, and she was out there on vacation with her girlfriends. Me and Dirty were onstage and we were rapping and it was raining. Das EFX was out there with us. The Fugees. And it was like, oh my god, Das EFX! Oh my god, the Fugees! Oh my god, Biz Markie! Oh my god, Funkmaster Flex! Look, look, oh shit! Oh shit! There go my man, Montell Jordan!

And then what *really* took me there, is when we was getting on the stage right after George Clinton, a living legend. George Clinton at one point told RZA that Dirty brought a cadence to music that nobody had ever done before. I don't know if Dirty even heard that he said that. But watching him perform, we freaked the fuck out. We stood there and watched his show and it gave us the inspiration of our lives.

And that's what I thought about when me and Dirty went onstage. These people are here, tuning in to see what are we about, what is our music about, why we do this, how does it make them feel when they hear it? The way we stomped our feet, shook our heads to the left and the right, pointed our finger somewhere for no reason. People just think, Oh, he pointed at me—I'm the next one to do it. We gave them inspiration. I would point my finger at people from the stage to let them know that they could do it too. And I still get e-mails from people saying, "You probably don't remember, but I was at an Ol' Dirty Bastard show and you pointed at me and ever since then I've been doing good with my music," and it's like, *wow*.

Final Thoughts

A lot of my teachers told me I'd never amount to shit, so I want to put out this message to the kids who might read my book: the only way to become successful in this game is to stay in school. Get your education first. Don't be disrespectful to your parents. Get your family and friends to support you 100 percent. The more people you get behind you, the stronger you become.

There will be unlimited stumbling blocks, but no matter how many times you feel like giving up, don't let it take away from your focus. I can't give up the dream because the dream came from two of the greatest of all time, and one of us is gone. To everybody who's trying to do music, please continue doing it. Don't give up your dreams. It's not going to happen overnight, but that doesn't make you less of an artist than the ones who blow up today. Remember, the ones who blow up today might not be here tomorrow. A legend to me is an artist who's been selling music over decades. I don't care if you had ten million fans when you started and today you got a hundred. You still have people believing in you, people who would still love to hear your album.

A lot of people in this industry didn't have hit records right away. Jay-Z didn't have hits right away. He had to listen. He learned from Biggie the way I learned from ODB, RZA, Busta Rhymes, Brand Nubian, MC Shan,

Final Thoughts

KRS-One, and Kurtis Blow. All of the great pioneers of this music made me who I am. As a little kid I used to lie in my bed and dream of being onstage one day hearing people scream my name. This is my destiny.

Go for your goals. If you're drinking or doing drugs you need to monitor what it's doing to your life. Look at yourself in the mirror when you wake up, and know and understand that you're hurting the people you care about and that one day you might not wake up to them.

Pray to God. Eat your spinach. Give a dollar to the needy. Play *Modern Warfare 3*. No matter how much you mad at the world, pick up a game controller and kill somebody online, not in real life. I play as AgentBMB if you wanna get your ass whooped.

By the way, the saga continues . . .

—BUDDHA MONK
WORCESTER, MASSACHUSETTS
DECEMBER 2013

Acknowledgments

Buddha Monk: I want to thank the main person that everybody should thank for this book, David Shanks, aka Traum Diggs. He introduced me to Mickey Hess. Thanks to you, Mickey. Without you it would not have been possible. I came to you to do a talk about hip-hop with your class at Rider University, and you took me to lunch at Houlihan's and we started writing a book. Thank you, Houlihan's.

I want to thank It Books and HarperCollins for giving me this opportunity, Denise Oswald for really taking the time to make this book what it is, and I definitely got to thank my number one girl, Barbara Braun, for getting me this book deal. Barbara, I want to thank you for believing in my book and believing in me and Mickey to make it happen. Thank you for giving me the opportunity to speak to the world. I thank you, Barbara, from the bottom of my heart.

I thank my mother, Carolyn Logan, for giving me life. She has been a great provider in words, wisdom, knowledge, understanding, and encouragement. What she couldn't give me in cash, she gave me in love. I want to thank my brother Born. To all my children (Shaquasha, Ellery, Monica, Jasmine, Jayden, Yakini, Zyella, and Nyala), whether you love me or you don't, I love you. This book will hopefully explain to you the struggles of my life to try to grow as a man and become a good father to you. I had a job that required me to not be home with you as much as I wanted to, and I'm sorry for that. I made mistakes and I wasn't there for you. I apologize.

I want to thank RZA, the whole Wu-Tang Clan—Method Man, Ghostface, Raekwon, GZA, U-God, Cappadonna, Masta Killa, Inspectah Deck—everybody who still brings me onstage and shows me love now that Dirty's gone. Popa Wu, all my Brooklyn Zu niggas, Mook, Hell Razah, Jimmy Kang. To my man Ron and all of them dudes who used to sit out on the stoop and give me advice about how to treat a woman and how to respect my elders. Miss Atlantis Price, my nephew Wasabi Fresh aka King Fresh, Senior Brown—I couldn't do this without you.

Mickey Hess: First and foremost, I want to thank David Shanks, aka Traum Diggs, without whom this book would not exist. Readers, finish this book and go listen to Traum Diggs. I thank Buddha Monk and Atlantis Price for inviting me into your home and trusting me to tell this story. It's not easy to put your life story in the hands of someone else. I thank Icelene Jones and the estate of Ol' Dirty Bastard, Messiah Jacobs, Young Dirty Bastard, Shaquita Jones, Taniqua Jones, Chandler Klang Smith, Deanna Nobleza, Jessica Kovach, K-Blunt, Mikki Pace, Shamika Mitchell, Lord Digga, Barbara Braun, Denise Oswald and It Books, Sean Carswell, Joe Meno, Todd Dills and Susannah Felts, Lauren Cerand, Stephen Dorse, Peter Richter, Steve Sachs, Ricky Lorenzo, Alexandra Sharry, Ashley Baker, Constantine Frangas, Cait Mawhinney and the baristas of Jersey Java, my Rider University students and colleagues (special thanks go to Robbie Clipper, Pearlie Peters, Arlene Wilner, Katherine Maynard, and Nowell Marshall), and all the guest speakers who've come to my hip-hop class (Prince Paul, MF Grimm, Greg Nice, Thembisa M'Shaka, K-Blunt, Count Bass D, and Masta Ace). Finally, I cannot underestimate the importance of Danielle and Coco Hess.

Notes

---

1. Rusty

5 *Dirty never accepted their split-up:* Cardwell, "The Life and Death of a Hip-Hop Jester."

6 *"I rap, but I sing":* "Ol' Dirty Bastard Gets Paid."

6 *"dying hound":* Henriquez, "Ol' Dirty Bastard + Dillinger Escape Plan."

6 *"His voice was unmatched":* Moss, "Ol' Dirty Bastard's Death Stuns and Saddens His Peers."

7 *"He was one of the best beatboxers":* Coleman, *Check the Technique,* 451–452.

2. Enter the Wu-Tang

17 *"When I first started producing":* RZA, *Wu-Tang Manual,* 190.

18 *"I'm Dirty because":* Nelson, "To Elektra, He's Not Just Another Ol' Dirty Bastard," 30.

3. In the Lab

27 *"I remember the first time I met Ol' Dirty":* Coleman, *Check the Technique,* 461.

31 *"I don't like to see":* Valdez, "Right and Exact."

31 *RZA says Dirty pulled:* RZA, *Wu-Tang Manual,* 122.

33 *"There was a mystique":* Coleman, *Check the Technique,* 459.

4. The Drunken Master

40 *"Dirty was making":* Ahmed, "Method Man Breaks Down His 25 Most Essential Songs."

42 *"I got Indian in me":* Valdez, "Right and Exact."

44 *Chris Gehringer, who was an engineer:* Mlynar, "Clan in da Back."

5. Ghetto Superstar

58 *"I wouldn't say my shit is New York"*: Nelson, "To Elektra, He's Not Just Another Ol' Dirty Bastard," 30.

6. Pupperized

61 *He rented them an apartment in Harrisburg, Pennsylvania*: Jenkins, "Looking for Jesus," 172.

65 *"have me sing a ballad"*: Nickson, *Mariah Carey Revisited,* 156.

7. That Old Good Welfare Cheese

69 *his father gave an interview*: McDonald, "O.D.B.'s Dad."

73 *"I'm not sure Ol' Dirty articulated"*: Hampton, "I Like It Raw," 63.

9. Escape to Willingboro

83 *Icelene told a reporter*: Martin, "Rap Star Ol' Dirty Bastard Charged as Deadbeat Dad."

84 *"I just want him to get some help"*: Jenkins, "Looking for Jesus," 172.

10. Restoration

91 *"There's nothing we can do"*: New York Times, "Harlem Mosque Sets Rap Peace Meeting."

92 *"Ol' Dirty Bastard is dead"* and *"I go to the schools in my area to talk"*: Valdez, "Right and Exact."

93 *"I can never be out of Wu-Tang"*: Ibid.

97 *He got arrested when*: Peterson and Claffey, "Rapper's Got the (Dead) Beat to Tune of 35G in Crackdown," 22.

12. Better Start Wearing Bulletproof

113 *"What the fuck did you do"*: Noel, "A Bullet for Big Baby Jesus."

114 *the NYPD Street Crimes Unit*: Kocieniewski, "Success of Elite Police Unit Exacts a Toll on the Streets."

115 *"They was lying"*: "Ol' Dirty Bastard Battles the Law: But Who Won?," 48.

117 *"Anyone who's been shot"*: Jasper, "Under Fire," 75.

13. Nigga Please

119 *"He's utterly dysfunctional"*: Jenkins, "Looking for Jesus," 172.

119 *"It took a while for* Nigga Please *to happen"*: Diehl, "Dirty Stories."

123 *"difficult for observers to tell"*: Huey, "Ol' Dirty Bastard (Russell Tyrone Jones)," 364.

124 *"Can you make the drugs disappear?"*: Hiatt, "Prosecutor: ODB Asked Cops to 'Make Drugs Disappear.'"

124 *"I love my son"*: Miller and Parascandola, "Bad Boy Rapper Back in Trouble on Drug Charge."

14. The Whole World Is After Me

127 *"Fuck all this Tommy Hilfiger"*: Bonanno, "Last Man Standing."

127 *"I came to West Africa"*: RZA, *The Tao of Wu,* 27.

128 *he told Ms. Howard she was the prettiest FBI agent:* Parker and Diehl, *Notorious C.O.P.,* 220.

129 *"Don't think that you're immortal":* Bry, "Hard Time," 114.

15. In a G Building, Takin' All Types of Medicine

135 *"See y'all in a couple of years":* Brennan and Frisby, "Dope or Bad Rap?"

135 *"He wanted to buy a house here":* Ibid.

136 *"His mental health is bad":* Fenner, "Rapper Faces Plea Deadline."

138 *"He got a raw deal":* Shaw, "Portrait of the Artist in Jail."

139 *"It's not easy for me":* Ibid.

140 *"I think the government is tryin' to set a nigga up":* Jenkins, "Looking for Jesus," 172–173.

140 *"was showing signs of schizophrenia":* Rush et al., "ODB's out of Jail, on Comeback Trail."

140 *In 2008 the biographer Jaime Lowe:* Lowe, *Digging for Dirt,* 188.

141 *"I was tired and was messing around with Ced":* Ma, "Black Elvis Is in the Building."

141 *He told* New York magazine *he was on Haldol:* Jacobson, "Older, Not Dirtier," 39.

142 *The U.S. Department of Homeland Security injects it:* Goldstein and Priest, "Some Detainees Are Drugged for Deportation."

142 *A 1974 ad in a psychiatry journal:* Haldol advertisement.

143 *"The testimony in this case":* Lowe, *Digging for Dirt,* 138.

144 *something that DMC said about his bandmate Jay:* Danois, "From Queens Come Kings," 66.

16. One More Chance

147 *"My world is full of a lot of temptation":* Cardwell, "The Life and Death of a Hip-Hop Jester."

148 *"This is his last chance":* (Inside) Out: ODB on Parole.

17. Free to Be Dirty

149 *"My mom is the only one who can check me":* Jacobson, "Older, Not Dirtier," 39.

18. If You See Dirty, Tell Him We Love Him

158 *Vanilla Ice says:* Lowe, *Digging for Dirt,* 209.

164 *"This loud, big man laying on the floor":* "Icelene Jones, O.D.B.'s Widow."

164 *"He really tried to change":* Woodberry et al., "ODB's Kin Saw Trouble."

19. Chamber Number 9, Verse 32

168 *"It is legal to walk down the street":* Bluuwise, "An African-American in Switzerland."

174 *"Dirty was real":* Emery, "Wu Fighters."

174 *"Tell Dame Dash that I'm looking for him":* J. Medina, Interview with Young Dirty Bastard.

176 *"I'd rather be sober":* Trykowski, "Meet Young Dirty Bastard."

177 *"I robbed that man":* Parker and Diehl, *Notorious C.O.P.,* 221.

Bibliography

Ahmed, Isanul. "Method Man Breaks Down His 25 Most Essential Songs." *Complex* magazine, Oct. 19, 2011. www.complex.com/music/2011/10/ method-man-25-essential-songs/ol-dirty-bastard-f-method-man-raekwon -raw-hide-1995#gallery.

Bluuwise. "An African-American in Switzerland." *Alicia Renee aka Blue Eyes.* http://bluuwise.wordpress.com/2011/08/09/an-african-american-in -switzerland/.

Bonanno, Jonathan. "Last Man Standing." *The Source,* Mar. 2000: 215.

Brennan, Chris, and Mister Man Frisby. "Dope or Bad Rap? Ol' Dirty Bastard's Known for Crime, Not Rhyme." *Philly News,* Nov. 29, 2000. http://articles .philly.com/2000-11-29/news/25613602_1_odb-russell-jones-drug -treatment-center.

Bry, David. "Hard Time." *Vibe,* Apr. 2002: 110–116.

Cardwell, Diane. "The Life and Death of a Hip-Hop Jester: Joy, Fame and Endless Struggle." *New York Times,* Nov. 18, 2004: B1.

Coleman, Brian. *Check the Technique: Liner Notes for Hip-Hop Junkies.* New York: Villard, 2007.

Danois, Erica Blount. "From Queens Come Kings: Run DMC Stomps Hard out of a 'Soft' Borough." In Mickey Hess, ed. *Hip Hop in America: A Regional Guide.* Santa Barbara, CA: Greenwood, 2010.

Bibliography

Diehl, Matt. "Dirty Stories." *Rolling Stone,* Nov. 11, 1999: 36.

Emery, Andrew. "Wu Fighters: Staten Island's Wu-Tang Clan Is Hip-Hop's Most Innovative—and Unstable—Group." *The Guardian*, Dec. 8, 2007: 4.

Fenner, Andrew. "Rapper Faces Plea Deadline." New York *Daily News,* Mar. 16, 2001: 2.

Goldstein, Amy, and Dana Priest. "Some Detainees Are Drugged for Deportation: Immigrants Sedated Without Medical Reason." *Washington Post*, May 14, 2008: A1.

Haldol advertisement. *Archives of General Psychiatry* 31, no. 5 (1974): 732–733.

Hampton, Dream. "I Like It Raw." *Village Voice,* May 30, 1995: 63.

"Harlem Mosque Sets Rap Peace Meeting." *New York Times*, Sept. 18, 1996. http://www.nytimes.com/1996/09/18/nyregion/harlem-mosque-sets-rap-peace-meeting.html.

Henriquez, Ryan S. "Ol' Dirty Bastard + Dillinger Escape Plan." *Popmatters,* Nov. 10, 2003. www.popmatters.com/review/ol-dirty-bastard-031024/.

Hiatt, Brian. "Prosecutor: ODB Asked Cops to 'Make Drugs Disappear.'" MTV News, Jan. 2, 2001. www.mtv.com/news/articles/1435861/prosecutor-odb-asked-cops-ignore-drugs.jhtml.

Huey, Steve. "Ol' Dirty Bastard (Russell Tyrone Jones)." in Vladimir Bogdanov, et al. *All Music Guide to Hip-Hop: The Definitive Guide to Rap & Hip-Hop.* San Francisco, CA: Backbeat Books, 2003: 364–366. Print.

"Icelene Jones: O.D.B.'s Widow." Interview. www.youtube.com/watch?v=iyGaHcVUWqc.

(Inside) Out: ODB on Parole. VH1 special, 2003.

J. Medina. Interview with Young Dirty Bastard. June 10, 2013. Shade45: Eminem's Uncut Hip-Hop Channel XL. XM Satellite Radio.

Jacobson, Mark. "Older, Not Dirtier." *New York* 36:33 (Sept. 29, 2003): 39.

Jasper, Kenji, et al. "Under Fire: A New California Law Restricting Civilians' Rights to Wear Body Armor Raises Issues of Safety and Police Behavior." *Vibe,* June 1999: 74–75.

Jenkins, Sacha. "Looking for Jesus." *Vibe,* Dec. 1999/Jan. 2000: 168–175.

Kocieniewski, David. "Success of Elite Police Unit Exacts a Toll on the Streets." *New York Times,* Feb. 15, 1999: A1.

Lowe, Jaime. *Digging for Dirt: The Life and Death of ODB*. New York: Faber and Faber, 2008.

Ma, David. "Black Elvis Is in the Building: A Definitive Talk with Kool Keith." *Wax Poetics,* Oct. 3, 2009. www.waxpoetics.com/features/articles/black-elvis -is-in-the-building.

Martin, David. "Rap Star Ol' Dirty Bastard Charged as Deadbeat Dad." Reuters, Nov. 14, 1997.

McDonald, Sam. "O.D.B.'s Dad." *Newport News Daily Press,* Dec. 20, 2004. http://articles.dailypress.com/2004-12-20/features/0412200023_1_hip-hop -cherry-jones-famous-son.

Miller, Adam, and Adam Parascandola. "Bad Boy Rapper Back in Trouble on Drug Charge." *New York Post,* Aug. 1, 1999: 7.

Mlynar, Phillip. "Clan in da Back: The Behind-the-Scenes Oral History of *Enter the Wu-Tang (36 Chambers).*" *Spin,* Nov. 5, 2013. www.spin.com/articles/wu -tang-clan-enter-the-wu-tang-36-chambers-oral-history/.

Moss, Corey. "Ol' Dirty Bastard's Death Stuns, Saddens Peers." MTV News, Nov. 15, 2004, www.mtv.com/news/articles/1493729/ol-dirty-bastards -death-stuns-saddens-peers.jhtml.

Nelson, Havelock. "To Elektra, He's Not Just Another Ol' Dirty Bastard." *Billboard* 107, no. 8 (Feb. 25, 1995): 30–32.

Nickson, Chris. *Mariah Carey Revisited: Her Story.* New York: St. Martin's Griffin, 1998.

Noel, Peter. "A Bullet for Big Baby Jesus." *Village Voice,* Jan. 26, 1999.

"Ol' Dirty Bastard Battles the Law: But Who Won?" *Vibe,* May 1999: 48.

"Ol' Dirty Bastard Gets Paid" (video). MTV News, 1995. www.mtv.com /videos/misc/101194/ol-dirty-bastard-gets-paid.jhtml.

Parker, Derrick, and Matt Diehl. *Notorious C.O.P.: The Inside Story of the Tupac, Biggie, and Jam Master Jay Investigations from the NYPD's First "Hip-Hop Cop."* New York: St. Martin's, 2006.

Peterson, Helen, with Mike Claffey. "Rapper's Got the (Dead) Beat to Tune of 35G in Crackdown." New York *Daily News,* Nov. 14, 1997: 22.

Rush, George, et al. "ODB's out of Jail, on Comeback Trail." New York *Daily News,* Apr. 4, 2003: 34.

Bibliography

RZA and Chris Norris. *The Tao of Wu*. New York: Riverhead Books, 2009.

RZA and Chris Norris. *The Wu-Tang Manual*. New York: Riverhead Books, 2005.

Shaw, William. "Portrait of the Artist in Jail." *The Guardian,* Mar. 21, 2002: 6.

Stein, Joel. "People: Citizen of the Week." *Time,* Mar. 9, 1998: 53.

Trykowski, Tyler. "Meet Young Dirty Bastard: Son of Ol' Dirty Bastard." noisey.vice.com/blog/meet-young-dirty-bastard-son-of-ol-dirty-bastard.

Valdez, Mimi. "Right and Exact."*Vibe,* Sept. 1997: 118.

Woodberry, Warren, et al. "ODB's Kin Saw Trouble." New York *Daily News,* Nov. 15, 2004: 5.

Young, Kevin. "Ode to Ol' Dirty Bastard." Performed at *Page Meets Stage,* Bowery Poetry Club, New York City, Oct. 27, 2010.

About the Authors

Buddha Monk has toured the world and worked with musicians from Brooklyn to Moscow. A singer, producer, and rapper, he toured and recorded with Ol' Dirty Bastard and Wu-Tang Clan from 1992 to 2004 and released his solo album, *The Prophecy,* in 1998. When Dirty died, in 2004, Buddha considered quitting the music business, but after a hiatus he returned through the underground circuit with one goal in mind: ensure that ODB's legacy lives on.

Mickey Hess is Professor of English at Rider University, where he teaches creative writing and Hip-Hop and American Culture. He is the author of *Big Wheel at the Cracker Factory* and *Is Hip-Hop Dead? The Past, Present, and Future of America's Most Wanted Music,* and the editor of Greenwood Press's *Icons of Hip Hop* and *Hip Hop in America: A Regional Guide.*